# Kanban

*A Complete Step-by-Step Guide to the Basic Concepts in Kanban*

# TABLE OF CONTENTS

# Introduction

I would like to thank you for choosing this book, 'Kanban: A Complete Step-by-Step Guide to the Basic Concepts in Kanban'.

Kanban refers to a tool predominantly used in organizations to reduce occurrences of obstacles during project completion. The word Kanban comes from Japanese terminology and roughly translates as: "billboard".

Kanban came into being during the 1940s and was introduced by Taiichi Ohno to enhance the work philosophy and output in Toyota. He found that store clerks restocked grocery items by the store's inventory and not the vendor's supply. And just about when the items were almost sold out, the clerks would order more of the same. Looking at the grocer's "just in time" delivery model, Toyota engineers began to rethink and redesign new methods to adopt a new approach known as Kanban to match the inventory with the demand for the product in order to enhance quality and output.

Toyota decided to adopt the system and implement it in their firm. They began to send cards to suppliers to inform them about the quantities needed, and the card was stuck back to the products when Toyota received them. Once the parts were put to use, the same card was sent across to the manufacturers to tell them that they were in demand again, thus simplifying the entire process and assembling the different parts on time.

The system gained popularity and is now part of many organizations across multiple industries. Kanban boards have now evolved into Kanban software. They let a manager and his team know exactly how a project is moving forward.

The boards serve as a reminder of what some of the obstacles are and how they can be dealt with. This makes it easier to move through the projects and finish them on time with quality output.

If you are on the lookout to adopt this system in your workplace to enhance productivity and output, then you have come to the right place. This book will act as your basic guide to the Kanban system and how it can be implemented to enhance productivity and output.

Kanban system serves as just a base for the company to come up with their own set of principles and practices that can be implemented to smoothen out project management. The system should be well understood by the people who will be implementing it in order to exploit its benefits.

This book will explore the basics of the Kanban system and how it can fit into the different departments in your organization, regardless of its size and industry. The system is also used to predict the outcome of a specific project being carried out through the implementation of statistics and predictors.

The Kanban system can revolutionize the way in which your organization operates and how projects are carried out and completed.

Thank you once again for choosing this book; let us begin!

# Chapter One

# What is Kanban?

The Kanban system came into being in the 1940s to manage projects and processes in a company. Engineers at Toyota implemented the process to enhance productivity and provide quality output to its clients and customers.

The Kanban boards were provided to the management to look at the progress of the project and how the work was moving along. The main intention of using the boards was to find any glitches in the system that might end up being obstacles and fixing them to improve the output.

## History of the Concept

The history of the Kanban system dates back to early 1940s. Taiichi Ohno is regarded as the father of the concept and happened to be a Japanese Industrial Businessman and engineer who worked for Toyota. He is said to have revolutionized the production system and made key changes that affected the quality of the output.

The Kanban system was designed to bring together the different elements of the project in order to understand the workflow and deal with any issues that might arise during the progress of the project. These issues could well limit the working of the project and end up delaying it.

Thus, Ohno wanted to introduce a system that could portray the progress of work and how the project was moving. It was possible to keep in touch with the progress of the project and how the different departments were doing.

Using the system made it possible to control the different departments and reduce some of the waste, such as the raw materials that were being used.

Toyota defined the system of Kanban as a relay system to standardize the flow of their different departments. They were inspired by the way in which groceries were delivered to them on time every time. The team had visited a grocery store known as Piggly Wiggly supermarket in the US, where Taiichi looked at how the shelves were stocked with the right number of products to match customer demand, and visual reminders were placed to keep stock of the products. The clerks would know exactly when to call in for more products to be restocked on the shelves.

The clerks made use of a concept known as JIT, or Just in Time delivery system. Toyota implemented the same in their company, more specifically in the manufacturing department.

Kanban started with knowing about the customer's orders and following it up with the production stream. Kanban was nothing but a card that would be issued with an inventory number on it that would be attached to the top part of the inventory.

Just before the specific part was being used or installed, the card placed on it would be pulled off and sent to a supply chain for another part. As per the system, a part was only ordered if a Kanban card was mentioned on it. This system therefore gained the name "pull system" owing to the pulling out of the cards.

The Kanban system predominantly controls the entire system, from the value chain from the supplier's end right down to customer requirements. It helps to take care of any issues that might come in the way of the supply chain and also reduce surplus items that might be present at varying stages of the production line.

The Kanban system needs consistent monitoring and attention to the different obstacles that might crop up during production management in order to enhance the movement of the process. All companies that adopt the system aim to attain a higher output with lower delivery times so that it is easier to hold on to existing customers and get new ones on board owing to the efficacy and quality of output provided.

It was a matter of time before other organizations took notice of the system and began implementing it in their organizations. The main aim was to keep track of the progress of the project and to enhance the output whilst not wasting resources.

Leaders such as Reinertsen, Dumitriu, and Anderson began adopting the system and applying it to their specific fields. Although their system had variations that were meant to cater to their specific needs, the basic structure remained the same.

The Kanban system was adopted by Microsoft in 2004 and was not implemented until 2005. The system was fully customized to suit the requirements of the company to maximize the efficacy to match the workflow and keep the business moving from strength to strength.

The system is now widely used in many companies including Spotify. They swear by the utility that the system provides in order to enhance the productivity and the impact that it has on the final output.

The system can be adopted by pretty much any organization belonging to any industry.

## What is Kanban all about?

The word "Kanban" comes from a Japanese word that roughly means "Billboard" and was introduced by Taiichi Ohno.

The concept was inspired by how supermarkets operate and only stock their shelves with items that will meet customer demands and can be restocked based on sales. That is, the number of products that are missing on the shelf, owing to their sale. It is a visual reminder of how many of the products need to be reordered or restocked. This ensures that there is a constant supply of the product without people having to wait for it.

The same concept can be extended to an organization where each process depends on another. Most organizations can be viewed as supermarkets where the inventory needs to be stocked depending on its use. The parts should be readily available to be implemented without the need to wait.

The system is simpler than it sounds and can be adopted by just about any organization to enhance output. It is all about knowing exactly how much inventory will be required in order for it to be consumed within a set number of days. This helps to know when new inventory needs to be ordered to restock it.

Suppliers will be made aware of the materials that need to be supplied based on the cards that are sent to them. This will help them match the demand and control their production and manufacturing limits. It will prevent them from having any surplus supply and maintain the right amount of inventory at all times.

The company does not need to worry about having surplus inventory that is not being put to good use or is being wasted. This helps to control spending and saving money.

Chances of too much inventory lying around and getting spoiled is also avoided. In effect, by engaging in Kanban, a company has the chance to make full use of their access to the right amount of inventory.

The Kanban system can be used to set limits for the level of inventory that is to be ordered and how much will be stocked, including the stuff queued for work in progress.

Imagine yourself standing in a supermarket where the queues are long and tiring. Same way, inventory at the organization should not queue up without being put to proper use. It can disrupt the functioning and create obstacles in the assembly line. By setting upper limits, it is possible to limit the length of the queue. And just like a supermarket, the shorter the queues are, the better it is for customers.

Toyota used cards to implement the Kanban system. It was the most accessible system that could be implemented at the time.

The system was developed to match the inventory with the demand. It was used as a means to assess demand, forecasting exactly how much inventory was needed to match the demand. Thus, the processing team would be handed the cards to assess the demand for the products. The supply chain received the signals to move according to the demand stimulus.

The main aim was to balance out the movement of the different processes involved in order to avoid bottlenecks or control them to an extent. It was important to strike a balance such that the stock was limited but it did not impact sales. This meant that the Kanban system had to be pushed in the right direction for it to succeed. This meant that there had to be strict rules that had to be followed for the system to work. Some of the rules were as follows:

- Kanban is indicative of both the sequence and the quantity

- Without implementing Kanban, there is no use of producing and transporting the items

- When the goods happen to move from one process to the next, they should have a Kanban

- The goods should not be passed if there are any defects and, by default, Kanban serves as quality control

- The lesser the Kanban involved, the more efficient the process will be

Essentially speaking, the Kanban cards served as a reminder for top up as soon as inventory started to deplete. It was the easiest and simplest way of managing inventory. It was not an easy task, as there would be several cards going around, but Toyota remained extremely efficient and managed to keep up with the system.

Today, the process of using Kanban is very different. Cards have been replaced by technology and it is much simpler to keep track of the movement of the system. There is no longer a need to depend on physical cards. Electronic messages are used that are easier to track and implement. They move faster, often within a flash, and are simpler to understand.

The system has made its mark on the IT industry and was developed by David Anderson. He used the works of Eli Goldratt, Peter Drucker, and Demmings to understand concepts such as queuing theory and flow to come up with it.

## The Three Bin System

Let us use a simple example to understand how the Kanban system works. It is one where three bins are used for the cards. One is somewhere on the floor of the factory, one is at the warehouse where the different inventory is maintained, and the final one is with the supplier.

The red cards stand for the supply requirement. The production staff uses these cards. Once all the cards have been used up, the empty bins are sent to the store to await instructions on what needs to be produced to meet demand.

The store then fills the bin with the Kanban cards and collects and sends the materials that match the cards. This in turn means that it requires more inventory from the supplier, and thus, the store sends the Kanban cards to the supplier who come up with the inventory or parts that are sent back along with the Kanban cards. This means that at any certain point in time, there will only be one empty bin.

This might sound easy but imagine the number of cards that actually need to be moved from one place to another. How many times have you ended up losing an important piece of paper and have then gone on the rampage to look for it? Similarly, an error in the information or a missing card can stir up a storm in a large-scale production.

But with the help of electronic cards, this problem was solved. There is no danger of losing a card with the electronic system. There is no need to worry about the cards going missing as they can be tracked or traced. The time taken for it to travel from one department to another can also be tracked. It will be much easier to transfer it electronically compared to manually. All it takes is following a digital map system.

As mentioned earlier, many top companies have employed this system in their firms to enhance efficacy and productivity. Some include Bombardier Aerospace and Ford Motor Company.

## Tallyfy and Electronic Kanban

Regardless of what your instruction or order is, it is very easy to handle it through Tallyfy in order to get the best results. In case something goes wrong on the way, you will find it very easy to track the issue or the reason for the glitch. You will know exactly what is interfering with the workflow and where the bottleneck lies. This helps to find a solution at the earliest before the issue blows up. It will be possible to trace the bottleneck in a matter of minutes, what would otherwise have taken weeks or even months. This type of control over the system and control in the hands of personnel involved can help to keep the Kanban system in check.

Companies can opt to have their Kanban system designed for them. All they have to do is state the requirements for the companies to curate the system specific to their needs.

# Kanban Method Principles

The Kanban method prescribes to a list of practices and principles that are needed to keep it moving smoothly. It also helps to tackle the workflow and help it remain free from disruption.

Its main aim is to smoothen out the different processes that are carried out in the organization and to successfully implement a consistent workflow free from bottlenecks and hiccups. The aim is to reduce the delivery time taken to deliver the final output and enhance the level of customer satisfaction.

Here is a look at some of the basic principles associated with the method.

## Foundational Principles

### Start with Whatever You are Doing Now
The Kanban system does not give you any setups or procedures to follow. The system can be overlaid on whatever it is that you are doing now to identify some of the issues associated with it and to introduce some level of change over time. This makes it quite easy to implement Kanban, as you do not have to make too many changes that can be difficult to adopt.

### Evolutionary and Incremental Change
The Kanban system is all about introducing small changes into the system and getting the team members to adopt the change. If bigger changes are made, it might find some amount of resistance from the team members and the organization in general. So incremental changes must be made for them to stick and revolutionize the way a company works.

### In Keeping with Current Roles, Responsibilities, and Designations
The Kanban method does not call for any radical changes in the structure of the organization. This means that you do not have to introduce any changes in existing functionalities, roles, and

responsibilities that may not be doing well. The system will be able to identify the different changes that are required and implement them so that it is easier to accept the changes by tackling the fear and resistance towards change.

### Promotes Acts of Leadership
The Kanban system promotes improvement in the organization and leadership acts that do not have to be performed by managers alone. People who are at different levels are made to show their leadership skills and introduce ways in which a change can be introduced in the systems. They are made to identify the different ways in which to improve products and services that can be delivered on time, every time.

## Core Practices Involved with Kanban

### Visualizing the Work Flow
When it comes to adopting and implementing the Kanban method, it is important to visualize the way in which the work will flow. The steps have to be visualized through the use of either physical boards or Kanban boards to find the steps that have to be taken to finish the work and deliver the final goods.

There are no specifics to how a Kanban board should be and can be either just a simple or complex system based on the teams that will be using it to deliver the end product.

Once the various processes have been visualized, you have to also visualize the work that is being done currently by the team in question. This can be achieved through the use of color notes to find the various levels at which work is being carried out.

The choice is yours to include different columns and colors for the different processes involved and what has been assigned to the different team members and the team as a whole. The color boards can be redesigned according to ones likely to bring about change in the systems.

Incoming work requests should also be visualized in order to carry them out effectively. When it comes to project work, criteria such as risk can prove to be precursors or markers for work to be classified. Some common metrics used to categorize risk include differentiators, spoilers, cost reducers, and table stakes.

Kanban does not specify any type of specific workflow. Thus, there is no way to categorize the requests. If there are five different departments from five different companies, then the data will be presented in five different workflows and will still be quite cohesive.

### *Limiting Work-in-Progress (WIP)*

When it comes to implementing the Kanban system, it is important to limit the work in progress. This will help the team finish whatever is going on before moving to a new project. This means that the team is only allowed to take on a new process when the work in progress is nearing completion. This will enhance the team's productivity and ring in more work.

It is usually not easy to find the progression of the work being currently carried out. You can consider beginning with no WIP limits and then look at how the team is performing under the Kanban system. If you happen to have a sufficient amount of data to define your WIP limits at all stages of workflow, then do so.

Mostly those teams that begin with WIP tend to limit their work to either 1 or 1.5 times the number of team members specified for the task.

It is best to limit the team WIP so that each member is able to finish the work on time, every time before moving on to newer tasks that have been assigned.

This will also tell the stakeholders about the customers that exist and the amount of work that is being performed by the team as a whole. It is therefore imperative to engage in careful planning when new tasks are being designed and implemented.

### Managing the Flow

It is important to manage the workflow when you have successfully tackled WIP. The Kanban system can help to manage teams and their workflow by highlighting the different stages involved in the process of the workflow and where the work currently stands.

The WIP limits that are set depend on how the workflow is being defined. Teams will notice the workflow and whether it is being completed on time within the WIP limits that have been set, or whether something is leading to the work being held up. This can affect the speed at which the work gets done and is delivered.

Kanban system can help to understand the system and introduce any changes to it in order to improve the workflow. It helps to understand how a task can be completed faster and how the time taken to deliver the end product can be reduced. It is important to consider the intermediate stages of work and solve issues from there in order to ease out bottlenecks.

Teams should analyze the time taken to solve issues in intermediate stages so that the work can progress smoothly. This is an important step of the process, especially when looking to reduce the time taken to deliver the final products or services.

Workflow improves and exemplifies a team's productivity and makes it much smoother for work to be carried out. It becomes more predictable and much smoother for the team to deliver the final result. The team will be aware of the time frame within which it has to finish the work. This will help the company know when a new project can be started.

## Making Explicit Policies

A part of the visualization process is defining policies that can explain how the work can be carried out. A team manager has to come up with policies that can define the work and how it should be completed. The policies should be prepared at a broader level, with the columns and colors predefined. These columns and colors are checklists that have to be ticked off once a particular task has been completed.

It is essential to make these lists for all the tasks that are involved and performed to help the team's work flow smoothly. Policies should pertain to defining when a task has to be completed and within what parameters.

One example of a policy that can be made explicit is defining done. A definition of done for every step of the way in the workflow process can mean before an item is pulled forward it should meet specific criteria. A few tools, such as LeanKit, will help with this process, and you will have the chance to use an electronic board. It can also be done using a manual board.

## Feedback Loops

Feedback loops are a very important part of every sound system and the Kanban method helps to encourage all teams to implement feedback loops in their systems. All teams must implement various forms of constructive feedback loops. The teams should look into the different stages of the workflow on the Kanban board and report the metrics to be used to improve any of the processes involved. Receiving feedback early in the process can often help teams. The manager will be able to identify the ways in which to deliver the work on time, every time, with just a few errors. Thus, a feedback loop will be critical to ensure the same.

## Evolving Collaboratively

The Kanban system aims to help teams introduce small changes to the system before big changes are introduced. This will make sure that teams will be able to handle the changes quickly. The system helps to use statistical methods to hypothesize and test the same in order to understand the final outcome.

The important task for the team is to look at the various processes involved and make changes wherever necessary. The final impact of these changes can be measured using a variety of signals placed on the Kanban boards. These signals can help to understand if the changes made really did help the process and whether they should be maintained.

The Kanban system can help the team find the vital information relating to the way in which each of the team members has performed and how the team has been doing as a whole. The data can be used to help them find newer metrics that can be used to understand the performances and introduce changes to the system, if required.

### Continuous Improvement

Kanban is a process that never finishes. It is an approach that needs consistent monitoring and analysis in order to improve it. it is essential to assess the flow of the project and eliminate bottlenecks. Thus, consistent monitoring is essential. Even if a firm does not manufacture tangible goods, the Kanban system can be implemented. Thus, services such as healthcare, software, and professional services can all use the Kanban system in their day to day working. The idea is to create a smooth flowing business without obstacles and reduce the overall cost of production.

## Kanban – Here to Stay

By now you understand what Kanban is and what it can do for an organization. There are some who think that Kanban is obsolete and does not really fit in with the types of organizational structures that currently exist, but this is not true at all!

Kanban, as a system, has evolved over time and continues to advance. It is now a pull system and not a push system. The system makes it easier to track the progress of a project and know exactly how specific departments are faring in an organization.

As technology advances, systems become more efficient. The same extends to Kanban, as the systems make it easier for management to track the work and the way in which the organization is moving forward.

There is no denying the fact that some companies have abandoned Kanban and moved on to other technologies to promote workflow. It is also a fact that most of these methods and technologies use Kanban as their base and, thus, Kanban will always remain relevant.

So, it is safe to say that Kanban will remain an important aspect of workflow management regardless of how advanced technologies become. The basics will remain the same. There might be some minor changes introduced to make the tools more powerful.

## Push Production vs. Pull Production

One of the main purposes of using Kanban systems is to pull the process to help a customer take what they want. The flow starts as a single part that is manufactured as per requirements, but this is not always a possible scenario without proper redesigning and investing. It is radically different from what companies are used to doing.

Traditional production systems go about their process by first scheduling then ordering raw materials and then manufacturing to create products based on forecasts of what the customers are expected to order. This is known as push production and is usually driven by the materials that are being used and the processes that are being controlled. This results in the production of products in large quantities and tying up of a large capital in WIP.

Pull production works the other way around and is all about a customer taking a product from the end of a production line to send a trigger for the production of the next part to begin.

For example, it is like how a supermarket will fill up empty shelves; the previous process in a flow will make a request for the parts that need to be processed from its preceding process. This process is controlled by using Kanban systems.

## How Does Kanban Pull Production Work?

In its basic form, a Kanban system is nothing but a signal back to the next operation to create the next part. This means that, for a simple process, having a single piece flow, the Kanban system operates in a simplistic way. Do not make the mistake of thinking that the production process is a simple one. Most processes cannot manufacture just one product at a time in an economic manner and will not be fast enough for quick changeovers. There will also be different production lines making many products that cater to different types of customers. All of this can make things a little complicated and will thus need a little thought to be put together for the design system to work smoothly.

So, whether you use the pull system or the push, the following rules must be implemented.

- The proceeding process collects products from the preceding process

- The proceeding process tells the preceding process what is to be produced

- The preceding process only makes what is required by the proceeding process

- None of the products can be made or produced without the permission of the Kanban system

- No defects should be passed on to the next process

- Reducing the number of Kanban in the system can increase the system's sensitivity to the alterations and is the best way to find problems in the systems and come up with solutions

It is important for the right environment to prevail in order to implement the Kanban system. The further you remain from the systems, the harder it will be for you to implement it.

## Regular Customer Demands

If customer demands are irregular, then it can be difficult to use Kanban cards. It will be like a supermarket where customers are irregular and thus unpredictable. The company might end up having more stock than required and the WIP levels will need some thinking.

## Product Variation

If you happen to make many products, then it is important to not have too much stock of each as you can end up having too much stock. The best way to deal with the burden is by ensuring that there are common parts between the products.

## Flow

It is all about organizing in order to control some of the chaos while using Kanban systems. Better organization will lead to better flow line or cell.

## Smaller Machines

The use of smaller machines can be much better than larger machines. Larger machines can end up in the creation of larger batches of products that can be tough to stock. It is therefore better to have smaller dedicated machines to control product flow lines.

## Quick Changeovers

Some machines and processes can take a lot of time to be set up, and this again can end up creating bottlenecks and a large stockpile. By implementing single minute exchange of die techniques, it is possible to bring about a change in this area.

## Repeatable Processes

It is important to maintain systems and operations in order for machines to maintain efficient Kanban systems. By using Total Productive Maintenance, it is possible to control the systems better.

## Repeated Suppliers

Suppliers are an important part of the process and are needed to make sure that they will be able to adopt the Kanban system for it to work smoothly.

If these conditions do not prevail then it does not imply that the Kanban systems cannot be adopted. It only means that you must put a little extra thought into how you will design the systems and how they will work. If there are irregularities in the demand and a lot of variations in the production, then it might require CONWIP systems compared to seen cards or bin systems. Unreliable machines might need bigger safety factors for the quantities that are to be used within the systems.

If you are just starting out with Kanban systems, you will have to do so with larger Kanban quantities and then reduce the stock in a systematic manner in order to get rid of some of the problems. By reducing the level of inventory, it is possible to get to the bottom of many issues that might be present in the system.

# Chapter Two

# How Kanban Works

The Kanban system can be extremely effective in helping companies enhance productivity and deliver better results at a faster pace.

The system can be modified to suit the specific needs of a company. A very simple form of Kanban is using grids. These grids can have a single row and multiple columns. The columns stand for the processes in which the workflows starting from the left and ending at the right.

If the team is working on more than one project or there are sub-teams working on different projects, then the one maintaining the board can use rows to separate the cards. These cards can be moved based on the progress of work and where they currently are in the project.

Once the Kanban board has been set up, the members visit the board from time to time to understand where they stand and move the cards to match their progress. The main motive is to pull the work towards the final column of the board that is labeled as "Done". When the team meets up at the board, they will discuss what card needs to be moved to which column. If a person is working on moving the cards and finds an obstacle in the way, then a meeting is called to resolve the issue.

## The Kanban Mind Frame

To exploit the full benefits of the Kanban method, a team has to invest in more than just a board and a few cards. The team must completely adapt itself to the system and work on their overall behavior, acceptance of the concept, proper implementation, and more

20

importantly, consistent upkeep. The project manager has to overlook the board in order to ensure that everything is going to plan. Here are some things to bear in mind while using Kanban boards.

It is important to eliminate multitasking. According to research, those who engage in multitasking end up dividing their attention, and this can cause tasks to slow down and lead to issues in the quality output of the project and also increase final costs.

It is important to limit the WIP so that multitasking can be cut down. One has to restrict the number of cards that are used on the Kanban board. It is up to the project manager to ensure that the tasks, projects and feature cards are not pushed on the board in the "Doing" column. Doing so might create a casual attitude in the minds of managers and lead to slowing down of the work.

It is more important to develop a culture of resolving issues for a team than engaging in finger pointing.

The project manager has to ensure that backlog is given priority and a dedicated backlog column is maintained next to tasks, projects, and other features that can provide value to customers and the business as a whole.

The Kanban system is an effective system that helps to finish projects on time. Just like lean tools, it will do best when it is adopted along with a mindset that caters to learning and improvement in the working systems. There cannot be just a single correct way to implement the Kanban system and many different factors can influence it. A team has to work on using the boards to suit their specific needs and improvise based on project requirements.

Kanban is a management system that is usually seen as being both quite revolutionary and non-disruptive in nature. This implies that the current processes can be improvised by introducing minor changes to the system. The risk that is proposed to the entire system can be reduced if the team introduces minor changes to the current workflow compared to major ones. This type of approach can lead to lower levels of resistance from team and customers alike.

An important aspect associated with Kanban is visualization. The team should be equipped to visualize the process of workflow and assess the way in which the work is moving within the organization. The best way to do this is through the use of visual cues or boards and differently colored sticky notes. The different colors of the notes will stand for different tasks.

Three different columns can be drawn out, where one stands for "to do", another for "doing", and the last one for "done".

This type of visualization helps to keep the entire process transparent, as it will be easy to track the progress of work and avoid any obstacles that might crop up. Kanban boards can be used to showcase how complex workflows can be visualized and assessed to determine how the projects will turn out.

The basic concept associated with Kanban pertains to how flow is established in the workplace. The cards used to represent this flow signify how smoothly the work is progressing without any blockages or time wasting. It tackles any hindrances that might be a part of the process and examines the basic flow of the work through the use of Kanban boards and cards. The system is designed to achieve a kaizen state of consistent improvement. The concept of flow is a critical aspect associated with the process of the work being carried out and how it can be improved to deliver better end results within shorter periods of time. It will lead the teams to decrease cycle times and enhance the quality of work by encouraging consistent feedback from customers and owners.

## Things Required

When you want to get started with the Kanban board, there are a few basic things you will need which have not changed since the time the system was introduced at Toyota. Here are the three main things:

### Kanban Board

The Kanban board is one that keeps track of the workflow of the project and is usually referred to as a workspace.

### Kanban List

The Kanban list is also known as a lane and is made up of a set of cards that are typically in the same stage of progress and placed in a column known as the Kanban board. It is the same as traditional projects referring to lists as to-do lists.

### Kanban Card

A Kanban card is a card that has items pertaining to the board and the list, and mentions things such as things to be done, products to be made, amongst others. It is better known as a task list in conventional systems.

Using these as a base, it is possible to come up with multiple Kanban systems that can cater to both specific and generic needs. How you use the boards can be limitless. It will be possible to come up with multiple boards to manage a company's different departments, including production, manufacture, and sales, amongst others.

The first board usually mentions the activities followed by the development team and keeps track of progress by moving the cards around on the different lists to do, doing, and done. The second board is all about the marketing team that divides the work and categorizes it in different columns, such as press pitches and internal promotion.

These are mere examples of how a company can use the Kanban system to organize the different processes involved. The core of the system will always remain the same and an organized workflow will be established.

## The Most Important Features of a Kanban Board

If you are used to using traditional checklist systems then you will be used to making lists, adding comments and notes, and checking off tasks that are completed. With a Kanban board, things work a little differently.

In order to help you understand the difference, and tell you exactly what Kanban board apps can offer you, here is a look at eight of the most common features. The names of these features and what they can do will usually vary from app to app, but the basic function will be the same across all apps.

### Moving Cards between Lists on the Board

One of the most common and prominent features is moving the cards between the columns on the boards. It is a feature that you will be using predominantly on any Kanban board app. Once you move an existing card on the board, you will be making space for new cards. Generally, the placement of the cards is moved around up and down a list, depending on the list. All you must do is place the cursor over the card in order to move it around or move it to a new location.

If you wish to move the card or copy it to a new location across boards then it can be done via the settings option on the board. Apps such as LeanKit will allow you to change up the entire layout of the columns such that it can be moved to a lower or a higher column. The choice is yours to experiment with the board and drag the cards wherever you want to place them without a break.

You will have the choice to look at the path that the card followed, and this can be done via the card's activity stream. Look for it by clicking on the back of the card.

### Invite Team Members to Kanban Boards to Assign and Subscribe to Kanban Cards

Just as in the case of traditional project management tools, Kanban board apps will let you invite other team members, clients, project managers, and customers, amongst others, to collaborate with you on a specific project. This is usually done on two levels, namely boards and cards. Each of these boards comes with its own settings and will allow you to invite members. For example, if you use the app Trello, you have the option of inviting another Trello user to the board. If you belong to a specific organization then you can find specific members to add to the list from the members in the organization. If you cannot find them by name, then simply add their email address and get them to join the same Kanban board as you. Once you add the person, they will be able to add cards to the board and also move them around, add comments, and edit the cards, amongst other things. They will also be able to keep track of the activities that are taking place on the board so that the project can be continued.

The cards on the board will have different members assigned for different purposes. Once members have been added, the task can be split between them. Once this is done, notifications will be sent to everyone based on the activities that have been assigned to each. If someone leaves a comment on the card, the app automatically sends a message to notify everyone about it.

If you are not a part of a specific task but would like to know of its progress, then you will have the option to "subscribe" to it so that you can know exactly where the project is. This will send you notifications of any activities that are taking place. If you think you do not have to follow the activity, then you can simply unsubscribe from it.

### Making Conversations on the Board
One of the main and most useful features of the Kanban board is being able to add comments to a project. If you are used to using Post it Notes to track your activities, then you would have to run to the board every time you wish to make changes on the cards. With online boards, you do not have to run anywhere and can make changes to the board with the click of a button.

Most apps give you the option of adding notes and attaching files related to the project. There is also an area provided where you can hold conversations with others who are a part of the project. When you have the conversation or leave a comment, you have the chance to mention other team members by using the "@" option to tag them, just like you would do on Facebook or Twitter.

In order to use these features, you have to click on an option known as a "card back" and can look for a link to it in the features column and simply click on the card to open it automatically.

### *Adding Lists and Tasks to Kanban Cards*

It is understood that projects require a lot of lists and tasks that need to be taken care of. These lists should be attached to the project so that it is easier to carry it out. On a traditional board, you would have to make the lists and attach them to the board, and it is quite difficult to manage two or three different lists at the same time. With the help of electronic Kanban boards and cards, it is possible for you to add as many different lists as you like. You can also choose from a list of predetermined checklists that are as follows:

- Initial pitch email

- Follow up information

- Media assets delivered

- Confirmed coverage

- Published coverage

Depending on the tools that you are using, the card will show you a completed percentage to help you track your progress on the board and tell you exactly where you stand. Just like the comments and descriptions that you can add, you can use the "@" option to mention others on the checklist. Apps such as Zapier use checklists to mention and assign roles to others in a workflow. Each card has an editing option on the checklist, along with three tasks, such as micro edits, macro edits, and newsletter copies that can be used along with the tagging feature.

### Including WIP Limits

Sometimes, the processes involved can become a little overwhelming when there are a lot of different tasks that have to be carried out at once. For this, Kanban apps allow you to cut down on or restrict the number of tasks that are being carried out at once. These are generally applied to a column as constraints to limit the number of cards that are added to a column. If a particular team is handling just one aspect of the project per week, then a WIP limit of about three or four cards can be added to the column with the task's name mentioned on it. These WIP limit tools can help an editor lay out the tasks on the Kanban board depending on the number of cards that should be added to the list. If you end up adding too many cards to the board then a message pops up saying there are already too many cards to add anymore.

### Tagging or Labelling Kanban Cards

A unique feature of using virtual boards is that it is easy to tag or label others. Labels are also referred to as tags and are a must-use feature for big projects. Depending on the app you use, this feature can help you tag or label people for the project to mention the work they are carrying out. The notes might be required to add a design or mention something to the development team in order to specify or outline a particular aspect. It can be one thing or multiple things that can help with the design element or other aspects related to the project. Labels and tags are usually not used across the board; only on a specific area on the board. It can be customized according to the board with differently colored labels and names to allow a smoother workflow.

### Putting Due Dates on Kanban Cards

An important aspect that people should bear in mind while working on projects is that it is essential to mention due dates for project completion. Due dates allow team members and project managers to know exactly when something needs to be completed. If such a date is not provided, then the chances are the project will not be completed on time, or worse, completed. Therefore, by attaching deadlines to the cards, it will be easier for the team to know exactly when the project needs to be completed and submitted. All you have to do is click on the due date button that is mentioned on the back of the card or under the clock icon that is present on it and select the date when the project has to be submitted. Most apps send across a due date notification so that the team knows when they have to submit it. To send reminders, the members have to subscribe to the cards. The tool will then automatically send reminders to the team members.

### *Viewing the Cards on a Calendar*

Kanban apps allow you to access a calendar. The calendar will have a record of upcoming schedules, deadlines, publishing schedules, press releases, delivery dates, amongst others. The calendar will help to add or move and edit cards on the board. If you have to reschedule something, then all you have to do is drag it over to a new date in the calendar.

These are some of the most useful features on a Kanban board.

## Best Kanban Board Apps to Choose from

Now that we have looked at what Kanban board apps can provide, we will now look at eight of the best apps that can be used by companies to track projects.

Visual Studio online is an app that gives you a Kanban view for work-related items. GitHub projects helps turn codes into Kanban boards automatically. Flow and Asana are task manager apps while Zoho Project is a project manager. Database managers like Airtable incorporate Kanban views to sort out tasks.

If you wish to go the traditional way, then you only need a white board, columns, and post-it notes to use as a visual reminder for where the tasks stand, and push tasks into the last column to signify completion.

# Ways to Test a Kanban Board

As you know by now, Kanban boards are used by companies to keep track of projects and their progress. These boards can be quite flexible in nature and can be used across different industries. They can also be used in meeting rooms and home offices, amongst others. To help you exploit a Kanban board's true potential, here are six of many ways in which a Kanban board can be used.

## *Managing Personal Tasks*

Up to now, we have discussed how Kanban boards can be used to collaborate with others for projects in order to finish them on time. Collaboration need not be the main motive for using these boards, and can also be used for solo purposes. It can be used by individuals to carry out their personal tasks. This can include coming up with to-do lists, mention doing lists, and also done lists. You can also add a backlog list to mention when a task or project will not go into any of these lists. Most of us rely on emails to inbox our checklists, but it can be a cumbersome task and time-consuming. With the use of a Kanban board app, not only will it be simpler but also convenient. The app can be pulled up at any time of the day to mark personal tasks. It will especially be easy to begin the day by making a checklist of tasks, just so you know how your day should go. You do not have to come up with a new checklist every day; you can recycle an old one by making a few changes to it. Trello and Zapier make for good options to choose from. Zapier will give you the option of recurring tasks that signify tasks that will be carried out regularly.

## *Building a Kanban Calendar*

There are dedicated calendar apps that let you track different events and tasks to complete. Using Kanban calendar can not only be easy but also help to manage your events in a better way. Apps such as Airtable and Trello will help you keep tab on your events and the dates by which they have to be completed. You can choose from the different list of options or mention your own events. It will help you keep track of any work that has been delegated and know exactly how to go about the different tasks. You can tag the person working on the project in order to track progress. Choose from macro edits, micro edits, and newsletter copy, and use the tagging option to tag the person responsible for the task. The calendar can be used to mention tasks well into the future. Although it is best to plan for just a week, you always have the option of planning much further.

### *Assembling Ideas on a Kanban board*

When it comes to assembling ideas that will be used for a project, it is important to highlight them properly so that it is easy to implement them. Future ideas can be listed on a Kanban board under different headings, such as possibilities or future ideas. They can be kept separate from current ones that can be mentioned under done. Many times, we end up having great ideas and then forget about them before writing them down. To prevent this, it is best to make a note of it on a Kanban board to ensure that we do not forget about it. Again, some of the best apps for this include Zapier. Use the integration feature to come up with Kanban cards that mention the ideas. You can integrate a variety of features, such as RSS feed, email suggestions, etc. to draw ideas from them and add it to a Kanban calendar.

### *Sharing a Map*

Most customer support apps come with tools that users can use to vote for new features to be incorporated into the app. This makes it easier for companies to know what people are looking for and what should be integrated into the system to make it easier for them to use. Suggestions include a shared inbox app that they can use to interact with one another. Trello can be used to exploit this feature. The Trello board is now public, and the requests made will be displayed publicly. This feature is a good option for those looking to conduct polls and garner public votes on individual cards to gather input from different individuals and users. This type of roadmap system helps companies know exactly what their customers are looking for. It makes it easier to incorporate it into the next product cycle. You also have the choice of filling in your own roadmap with ideas using Zapier to create cards on your Kanban app using slack messages and Evernote asana projects, amongst others.

### *Tracking Sales Pipelines using Kanban Board*
An important app to have to manage your sales is a CRM app. It stands for customer relationship management system, which helps to keep your team in check with sales. All you have to do is use spreadsheet CRM or contact-centric Kanban boards.

Many CRM and sales pipeline boards exist, and it is up to you to choose the right one for your company. Not all will make for the best choice and it is important to look up the different features to know whether it will be a good fit. What will work for a small team might not work for a big one, and vice versa. It is therefore best to choose software that is specifically aimed at your needs. Trello makes for a good option if you wish to track sales pipelines using Kanban boards. The sales team will know what is going on and what needs to be done at what point in time.

Most apps provide flexible features that can be modified to your liking. Nothing is too rigid, and everything can be customized to suit your specific needs. The system will respond to your specifications based on how you want it to function. Zapier makes for a great choice, too. It can help to convert emails, contacts, and proposals into Kanban cards and can also notify when cards or contacts have reached a specific stage. It can be used to pull up leads.

### *Hiring with Kanban*
It might be a headache to sort through applications when you wish to hire personnel. There might be just too many to go through and sorting might prove to be a headache. In order to resolve this issue, all you have to do is add all the applications to your inbox to make it a bit more manageable. You will need an application tracking system that can help organize the applicants and assign members of the team to hire people and make it easier for them to access relevant information.

There is built in software available for the task, like Breezy, that can be used along with Kanban boards. Zapier can help you with the same.

To start with, all you have to do is set up an inbox that you can name as a hiring inbox using your Google app account and use the Kanban app to come up with cards from every new email received. Use the subject of the email to serve as the title of the card and attach a resumé to pull the email body, the contact information, and other such details that can be added to the card's description. Make use of columns to make a note of the different hiring processes. It might not seem like a conventional tracking system but can help to keep the pathways clear and prevent emails from overflowing.

As you can see, Kanban systems need not be limited to tracking a specific project's progress alone and can also be used to serve many different purposes.

# Chapter Three

# Kanban in Manufacturing

It is important to implement a successful Kanban system for manufacturing and inventory management. The system can gradually help to improve the overall function of the project. All business functions including manufacturing can greatly benefit from the use of Kanban systems.

The Kanban system is a type of manufacturing system that can be used in the management of supply chain components through the use of instructions cards that can be used in line with the production unit. It is meant to be used as a pull production control system that is widely used for a set of circumstances. Better known as PPCs, this system is controlled from the floor by pulling materials as and when needed. Which system to use should be decided based on the kind of inventory that is being pulled during the process of production.

As mentioned earlier, Toyota used grocery store cases in the 1940s to understand the Kanban system that is predominantly used these days. Its base lies in Japanese roots, where the supply of components is controlled by using instruction cards along the production line.

## Kanban System in Manufacturing

Kanban systems can help to relay messages that are needed to replenish or produce an item. The system is mostly used during the production process and is also prominent in manufacturing units that use lean manufacturing practices to plan the production and procurement of raw materials. Kanban systems are usually common in

33

manufacturing plants, as there can be many different components required to process products and provide JIT delivery.

The main types of Kanban systems are as follows:

### Kanban Stock Squares

Kanban stock squares refers to markers used in application where inventory of stock such as boxes and pallets are stored on the factory floor. Most of the parts will be large, and need to be used at a certain stage of production. These systems are easy to integrate using the first in first out system, and can be used where there is no safety stick level needed.

### Kanban Inventory Containers

Kanban system containers are mostly used for small components that are used in the production line and batch production. These containers are usually used to store a certain number of items that are needed to complete a specific batch of activities.

### Electronic Kanban Systems

Electronic Kanban signals are required in applications that make use of electronic signals and are a part of production management software. Some of them include liquids, grains, and inventory systems.

## Kanban in Lean Manufacturing

Kanban is usually considered a lean production and eliminates labor and inventory waste. PPCS is a way to cut down on waste by managing the production and supply of things as per their demand. This means that the items are made as per the number that is needed based on market demand, as opposed to the usage of forecasting methods. In order to train employees in the Kanban method, it is important to have some program trials. With the use of instructional cards, signboards, and visual records, it is possible to know about the inventory. This helps to resolve and streamline processes faster.

Kanban systems are based on actual customer orders and are not on forecasts in ERP systems and facilities, where Kanban is usually implemented. Stock inventory is mostly based on the orders that have been placed by customers. That is, products are pulled from production based on customer demands. The use of visual markers helps to monitor the inventory, and it is possible to see exactly how many customer orders are being placed and when they are being placed. Once Kanban has been implemented, most facilities do not run out of materials and provide cost-effective solutions.

## Advantages of Kanban in the Manufacturing World

Kanban is used in lean manufacturing firms, as the main goal is to get rid of waste, thereby making factory floors reduce unused materials and extra stock. Kanban systems usually offer a lot of advantages, such as reducing waste and decreasing the costs involved in WIP. Here are some of the advantages provided by Kanban systems.

- It can help to lower the overhead costs of production

- It provides managers progress reports

- It gives people more control

- It can help to standardize production goals and increase efficiency

- It helps to improve flow and teamwork and how responsive a company is towards customer demand

- It can help to prevent over production of goods that can lead to a reduction in the waste and redundant inventories by almost 75% in some industries

We will look at these in detail in the next chapter.

## Role of Kanban in Operations Management

Kanban usually helps to improve operations by lowering inventory, and also improves output by fixing a shortage in inventory. As per the two-bin system, Kanban systems help to draw in inventory from one bin while the other bin will contain the inventory required to cover production until the first bin is refilled.

Let us say, for example, a company manufactures juicers. The company needs to store juicer motors in their warehouse. If they need 1500 motors per week, and it takes two weeks to get a fresh set of motors, then the management will need a backup of around 3000 motors at all times to ensure that enough motors are available in case of an emergency.

As soon as the last box of motors has been used, the people in the production line have to raise their inventory card to the purchasing personnel to order a fresh stock of motors. While awaiting the fresh stock of motors, the spare 3000 motors will be used.

## Essential Metrics of Kanban System in the Manufacturing Industry

When it comes to the manufacturing industry, people are usually bombarded with data, therefore making it difficult to filter information that is important to know what issues should be tackled. This can make organizations rely on BI programming applications in order to find performance indicators. These indicators are monetary and non-monetary measures that can help to assess the quality of output and the shortcomings in the organization to know whether they are in line with business agenda.

Here is a look at the different key performance indicators known as KPI

- Lead-time refers to latency between the start and execution of a process. If, say, the lead time between the placement of an order and the delivery of the product varies depending on the size of the product and the manufacturing procedure

- Cycle time refers to the time that is taken to deliver a product from when the work was started

- Throughput is used to measure how many products are being made using a machine line, unit, or plant over a specific period

## Common Types of Kanban Cards in the Manufacturing Industry

Here are the six main types of Kanban cards used in manufacturing:

- Withdrawal or Conveyance Kanban Cards

- Supplier Kanban Cards

- Emergency Kanban Cards

- Express Kanban Cards

- Production Kanban Cards

- Through Kanban Cards

Many organizations use Kanban systems to enhance productivity. The above is not an exhaustive list, rather a list of the most common types of Kanban cards that are used in manufacturing. Let us look at each of them in detail.

## Production Kanban

Production Kanban is the first type of Kanban that is implemented and can offset upstream processes to come up with and restock items through downstream processes. Production Kanban replaces standard production orders in an MRP push system. By implementing this system, a company can change up processes to pull systems information, including upstream process, downstream processes, part name, inventory number, shelf life, container quantity, cycle time, amongst others.

You are bound to find production Kanban in the form of Kanban boards, Kanban post, and upstream processes, amongst others.

If Kanban is stored as an attachment, it means there is no call to action required for the production process. When Kanban boards are used it means downstream processes have been removed and used from storage and have to be replenished. If production Kanban is in upstream process, it means fabrication has started or is about to start. The production Kanban system is usually made up of an exhaustive list of tasks that have to be completed to make sure the product is delivered on time. The information delivered through this process usually pertains to the materials to be used and other information needed in the production line. The system helps to begin with the production process and the processes to be followed for production.

## Withdrawal Kanban

The next type of Kanban card is known as withdrawal Kanban. It is mostly used to authorize the transport of items from one process to another. It is used at supermarkets in order to track products, give and receive information, and assess lead and cycle times that do not respond fast enough to downstream demand. In order to pull products from supermarkets, downstream processes make use of withdrawal Kanban. Once the items are pulled, production Kanban are placed on the Kanban boards and withdrawal Kanban are attached to the items to transport them back to the downstream process.

Withdrawal Kanban are usually found in a few places, namely items in transit, items awaiting processing at the downstream process, and items awaiting withdrawal. Withdrawal Kanban is usually the same as production Kanban except for two differences, namely the number of withdrawal Kanban that is needed to trigger off production Kanban information; value streams have longer cycle times or larger batches and are more likely to trigger withdrawal Kanban compared to production Kanban. This is owing to single withdrawal Kanban not being suitable.

At times, a specific number of withdrawals Kanban needs to be assembled on the Kanban board or the Kanban post before production, Kanban can be offset. This specific number is usually based on the analysis of downstream demand and the capacity of the upstream. The second figure that is a part of the withdrawal Kanban stands for is a measure of the number of items that should be moved.

In place of loose cards, some companies choose to attach Kanban cards to the transport carts or containers. This is done to constantly transport items. Through this technique, companies can reduce the chances of their cards getting lost in transit. This system is therefore alternatively known as a conveyance card Kanban system. If one or more cards needs to be moved from production to another department, then this system is preferable. It is used for signaling purposes. The cards that are used are all connected to various tasks that are being carried out in the factory. As soon as the task is completed, the cards are promptly returned.

## Emergency Kanban

Emergency Kanban is a system that is used to replace any damaged part or to signal that the quantity of the product needed to manufacture has increased or reduced in number. Most firms use this system when a specific part of the system is not functioning properly, or how it is supposed to function when changes have been introduced.

## Through Kanban

Through Kanban refers to a system that comprises production and withdrawal Kanban systems. Both these systems are implemented in places where workstations are placed adjacent to one another. The system is usually used to speed up the entire process. Say, for example, a factory has its production area right next to the organizing area; the through Kanban system will work on both over the production queue.

## Express Kanban

Express Kanban refers to a system where there is a shortage of parts in the system. The systems send signals to the different teams to increase the number of parts needed to complete the processes. The system tries to make sure that manufacturing and production of the products moves smoothly and are not slowed down. These systems are alternately known as signal Kanban systems, as they trigger off any shortage of purchases.

## Supplier Kanban

Supplier Kanban refers to a communication with external components, such as suppliers. This Kanban is usually the last one to be implemented, as it needs the supplier to be able to use the system internally. There must be well-established and smooth internal operations in place in order for this system to be implemented efficiently and before the system is taken up to the supplier. If the supplier needs assistance, then it is important to have knowledge on the system's functioning in order to help them out. Just as in the case of other systems, the demand should be based on the supplier's capacity. The supplier's capabilities have to be assessed when delivering the schedules and the quantities. Supplier Kanban is similar to withdrawal Kanban and both require replenishment of spare parts. The only difference is that it relies on communication with elements that are outside the organization. Information that is usually on a supplier Kanban card includes the supplier's inventory number, the quantity, the company from where it is, the delivery location, the shelf location, the contact number, and name, amongst others. To put it simply, the supplier Kanban is for a company or an individual from whom materials are sourced to make various products. The system moves towards suppliers and is usually seen as a representation of the manufacturer.

These are the different types of Kanban cards used in a manufacturing firm. These are used to enhance productivity and cut down on unnecessary costs.

# Chapter Four

# Benefits of Using Kanban Systems

Taiichi Ohno introduced the Kanban system in 1940s to enhance productivity in Toyota. He was inspired by the way in which products were restocked in a department store.

If a company focuses on managing work in place of managing people, then it helps to create a balanced atmosphere where creativity takes center stage and the true potential of the firm can be unleashed. This strategy is usually seen as being non-intrusive and easily adopted by all types of organizations to manage work with its structure.

Here is a look at how Kanban systems can help an organization.

## Emphasis on Value

The Kanban system is not just a method that can help to manage the flow of a project, but also serve as a decision-making tool that can be quite powerful in nature. The system is designed in a way that helps an organization make decisions that are specific to the goals that the organization is after. These goals are prioritized and implemented to attain best results. The main aim is to work on putting out results that are free from errors and helps to keep them ahead of the competition.

As per Don Reinertsen, a company must calculate the costs of delay in the production of a product. An organization should also try to discover what the costs are to implement a specific feature over another and whether this can help to set the organization apart from its competitors within its industry. Organizations have to also calculate any delays in the usage of one specific feature over another.

## Visibility

Most work that is carried out in an organization is usually done under covers and is thus imperative to be a lot more visible to the people at the forefront of the organization and to its customers. This is an important feature of Kanban. Kanban boards are usually used as a platform to provide information to assess the progress of a particular project, and to find and root out any bottlenecks and obstructions that might come up on the way. This information should be made available not just to members but also outsiders, including shareholders and customers. This will make it easier to access and transfer information. It can help the organization understand the actual work that is being carried out and how it is prioritized.

## Reducing Context Switching

The Kanban system takes care of the number of work items that are being carried out by the employees and is reduced to WIP limits. This type of system helps to deliver work and is high in priority and value, which increases the overall value of the business. Kanban systems can prevent teams from being burdened through the use of WIP limits. A member can start a task only after another has completed his. The basic principle that it adheres to is: stop starting and start finishing. This system helps teams remain focused on downstream activities.

## Enhances Collaboration

When it comes to organizational set up, most departments in an organization are usually isolated from one another. This can lead to a number of discrepancies owing to miscommunication. There can be times when there is a miscommunication between delivery teams and product managers. All this can be fixed with Kanban systems. Kanban systems promote integration into developmental value systems. It is nothing but a pull-based system that helps to bring together the different departments in an organization by pulling down its walls and resulting in a cross-department collaboration. This type of a transition can assist teams when sharing knowledge and information, and to collaborate and establish communication with each other.

## Reduction in Redundant Activities

Sometimes, project managers tend to focus exclusively on timelines and not on the process queues, as the former can be set in their thoughts. They make use of Gantt charts and other such documents to assess timelines for all the members on the team. What a lot of project managers do not realize is that they have to take care of the uncertainty and not just the planning aspect. A lot of project managers take the initiative to design activities to enhance timelines and undertake project risks in order to increase process queues. The Kanban system promotes WIP limits that are capable of making the system a pull-based one and thus allows organizations to maintain reliable and consistent ideas that are capable of delivering end results on time, every time. This will make sure that redundant work is eliminated, therefore reducing the number of queues that need to be deployed. A few upstream activities, such as workshops and business cases, will take place on demand, and thus project managers will be required to make decisions on time. Kanban also helps to co-ordinate activities that are relevant and validated to be prioritized across the Kanban board.

## Sustainability

Kanban systems help to manage work at a sustainable level. They reduce the level of stress and frustration and tackle a lack of commitment, therefore increasing the amount of work that is put out by employees. The WIP limits that are set help to control the speed at which a project operates. It is therefore used to enhance creativity. The teams involved will not commit to a process and break a promise. They will come up with out of the box ideas and solutions to issues, thus lead to fewer quality issues.

## Quality Enhancement

When it comes to making a business a success, it is imperative to focus on the quality of the output. It can result in the successful delivery of end products. If there are damages, then they can affect the team's output. By controlling them, it is possible to enhance the output and take care of any quality issues that might crop up right at the beginning in order to increase productivity. There can be different types of activities, such as collaborative analysis and documentation of high-quality software. Some of the principles of the Kanban system help to enhance professional quality and unify standards amongst project managers, customers, stakeholders, and others. This software helps to define principles at every stage of the process.

## Improving Morale

The Kanban system helps to instill a sense of morale and allows teams to perform under traditional setups to control some of the strategies that are involved. All the members in a team must come up with a schedule of their own in order to manage the workflow and remain cohesive with their managers. All members need to provide the final output on time by working rapidly at a steady pace to generate a concept known as good stress, or eustress. Kanban helps all members to manage their stress, therefore making them comfortable and helping to unleash their creativity.

## Product Obsolescence

When Kanban systems are used, there is no need for component parts to be delivered just before they are implemented, and this helps to reduce the storage space that is required. If the component or product has to be upgraded, then the upgrade can be made a part of the final product as soon as possible. There will be no storage of products that are obsolete and redundant. This goes well with the Kaizen system of improvement, where products can be upgraded on a steady basis and can be incorporated into products that do not have obsolete components.

## Storage Costs

The Kanban system is one that helps to reduce products and components that are scrap or waste. It helps to prevent overproduction of raw materials, as they are not required until implementation, thus resulting in a reduction of storage costs.

## Production Flexibility

If there is a reduction in the demand for a particular product, then the Kanban system makes sure that you are not housing extra stock. This means that you have flexibility to respond to a change in demand. Kanban systems also give you the flexibility in production lines. Supply chains do not lock in production lines. They can be accessed and switched according to the demand for a product. There will always be limits on the machines and the equipment, and also the skills portrayed by the employees. The supply of excess materials is eliminated.

## Increased Output

In case of a problem in flow of Kanban cards, there will be a problem with the production. The cards will highlight the problem much easily, thus making it possible to correct them as soon as possible. Kanban can help reduce waiting times, therefore making it easier to access supplies and break down barriers. This can result in an increase in production through the use of the same number of resources.

## Total Cost Reduction

With the help of Kanban systems, it is possible to reduce the total costs involved. It does so by controlling different factors, such as prevention of overproduction, development of flexible workstations, reduction in scrap and waste, reduction in cycle and lead times, and in costs of logistics, reduction in overhead costs and stock costs, resource saving through streamlined production, and reduction in inventory costs.

## Kaizen Culture

A kaizen board helps to manage teams through controlled queues that need shorter buffers. Pull--based systems help to tackle bottlenecks, obstacles, impediments and inefficiencies, amongst others. That can be a part of the delivery systems. There might be some issues that have to be identified and tackled in order to prevent the project from stalling. Using these queues, the Kanban system implements Kaizen, a concept where teams are taught to improve constantly and tackle issues that are present across the board.

## Predictability

Kanban system move past queues and lists that are found on a board and help managers forecast issues based on statistical data. This can help to reduce the risk involved in making guesses and make delivery times more predictable. After all, it is this predictability that helps to sustain a company and keeps it going. This can not only impact the cost of production, but also allow managers to be prepared for anything that comes their way in terms of varying demand. The team behind Kanban must ensure that they are on top of the system and calculate everything to assess delivery time. It is important to identify processes that are redundant and eliminate them so that no time is wasted. A manager has to inform the team about the limits that have been set in order to make the production more predictable.

## Work Visualization

Lean Kanban is used to translate production planning into visual Kanban boards and cards or electronic signals. A system map is employed to know what the specific system needs. Team members can see whatever the production is planning by looking at the Kanban boards.

## Reduction in WIP

A Kanban system is built to balance individual work cells to pull customer demand by making use of Kanban precursors such as boards and cards. A lean flow will help to reduce work in progress that is created using batch sizes that are much bigger than customer orders.

## Moving Work

A balance is achieved in the flow by assessing the rhythm of the customer's demand and adjusting specific work cells. This is done to achieve a balance in product flow. Team members will have a steady and even workflow that can satisfy their customers and also the management.

## Work Flow

Having a steady and balanced product flow doesn't just improve the final output but also proves to be a cost-effective option. It helps to steer clear of chaotic systems that are usually made of larger batches. The entire system will come together as one and reduce the stress levels that are undertaken by employees. This will promote a peaceful and calmer atmosphere within the organization.

## Work on Demand

As and when orders come in, it can trigger off the system to come up with the next batch of products. A system that is balanced will only come up with the right number of products needed to meet customer demands.

## Production Planning

Production planning can help to reduce Kanban size based on a change in market conditions. It is possible to have a balanced workflow that can help turnaround time by removing rushed orders that are seen as a problem associated with traditional production systems. This means that most orders are expedited as soon as workflow balance is established to meet customer demands.

## Planning Purchases

It becomes much easier to make purchases through the implementation of production planning. Kanban systems can be made simpler by using Kanban that are programmed to send purchase orders automatically to suppliers. It can be further simplified with e-Kanban systems.

## Customer Satisfaction

After all, the main aim of a business is to increase customer satisfaction. With the use of Kanban systems, it is possible to meet customer demands on time and provide quality output. As mentioned earlier, Kanban can serve as a quality control tool and thus will ensure that no defective pieces are sent out to customers. This can give your company a competitive advantage.

## Adaptability

As you know, Kanban is all about using visual cues to communicate. It can fit into pretty much every department. Right from marketing to production to sales, everybody can use the boards. This makes it ideal to be implemented across all departments.

## Consistent Improvement

One principle that is a big part of Kanban is that there is focus on continuous improvement. The system of visual management makes it easier to review the different processes involved and streamline the workflow.

## Level of Response

The faster the response, the better it is for the business. The Kanban system was designed to produce on time delivery. This means that the level of response is much higher, making it possible for a business to maintain agile workflow.

## Less Distractions

Kanban systems help teams to limit WIP, and thus encourages them to put out more output. Teams will find it much easier to finish their work and get a project across the finish line. There will be fewer distractions caused by multitasking, which leads to a better output. This type of collaboration and focus will lead to better results.

## Team Empowerment

The right Kanban system can help empower your team and share responsibility by moving work faster and finishing it. Kanban systems help to empower teams and make them make faster decisions that can push the project ahead with out of the box thinking and greater efficiency.

## Establishing Perfection

Using Kanban systems can help to focus on improving the system and enhancing responsiveness to problems. It means that projects that are fully seen through will have fewer errors and need less work. It will help to put control back into the hands of the project manager, therefore leading to more predictable outcomes.

There is a plethora of benefits associated with using Kanban systems. If you wish to implement one, then make sure you do your due research first to ensure that you are going for the right one. Based on your budget, shortlist a few systems and go through a demonstration to understand it better.

# Chapter Five

# Project Management and Kanban Systems

Project management refers to running an enterprise or checking off tasks from a checklist. The basic idea behind project management is to carry out tasks smoothly in order to complete them on time. The concept remains universal, regardless of the scale of the project.

It is a great idea to use a Kanban system in project management. Those who do will associate project management with visual management. It is obvious that nobody will have an idea of the progress of a project if there is no visual representation of the progress. And thus, it becomes more important to have cues in place that can help to understand where a certain project is headed. It is important to organize in order to achieve goals.

Software projects are usually defined as complex ones where projects can be imposing. The project manager will have a tough ask and is required to fulfill a multifaceted role. He must manage teams, take care of the budget, plans, and also assess the risks involved. The customers and stakeholders have to be kept in good books and sub-contractors have to be dealt with.

In order to take care of these diverse tasks, most companies go for project management implementation. Despite a good plan in place, it is still possible for the project to fail. As per studies, despite best efforts, only about half the projects that are undertaken are completed on time and within the set budget. It is believed that this trend is only growing worse with time, where managers are unable to complete tasks.

But with the implementation of Kanban systems, not only will it be easier to finish projects on time, but it will also save money while doing so. Here is a look at the concepts of Agile and SCRUM.

With process centric PMMs there is always more emphasis on being able to deliver specific requirements than delivering quality and value. With the use of SCRUM, a concept that emerged in the 1990s, people turned to Agile. The focus started becoming too much on teamwork and project management took a back seat. At least that was the case in theory. SCRUM as a concept usually works with a set of predefined roles and events and makes use of specific vocabulary.

But, SCRUM is not regarded as the solution to project-based problems. There are certain aspects that can influence the success or failure of SCRUM, and they are as follows.

- The maturity of the company and the understanding of agility

- The overall maturity of the team and the level of competency

- Allotting members to different projects

- Owning a project effectively

- The level of transparency that exists and visualization

These are the main requisites that must be met for SCRUM, but hardly ever are. The system can be transparent, but not everyone is a fan of it. Some might feel like everyone is exposed to everything and there are open discussions and debates on the same.

SCRUM can be tough to use in organizations that promote intense command and control. It can pose a challenge to scale down SCRUM and bring it down to a certain level and how risks and interfaces should be managed between different teams working on the same product. SCRUM can work well on smaller projects, as it does not do well with larger programs.

To narrow it down, traditional methods have not been successful in giving us the desired results, nor has SCRUM. They leave behind a few challenges.

## Kanban for Project Managers

The Kanban system can provide a solution to prior problems. One reason why people adopt it is because the system keeps up with an organization's current titles, roles, and hierarchies. Kanban can be referred to as a mindset over a method.

Kanban helps to begin work on the important bits first. This means there is more time to tackle whatever is important and then move on to other aspects. As we read, there are a few basic principles associated with Kanban that make it a great system to adopt. These are aspects, such as visualization of work, managing the flow, improving the collaboration, implementing feedback loops, amongst others.

There are a few parallels with SCRUM, such as the visualization and feedback, but the approach is not the same. Kanban allows you to work on different issues on the same board, and your focus will be on finishing tasks, namely the philosophy of stop starting and start finishing.

This philosophy is quite important because a lot of projects are not completed owing to glitches that can occur in the final stages.

Kanban helps you remain organized and systematic, and does away with task lists, email lists, to-do lists, and others.

Kanban can be implemented to fulfill all types of work, including technical work, repetitive work, working on deadlines, and unexpected work.

The main idea is to limit WIP to control it. It is important to visualize subcontractor work and meet deadlines. This can give you a bird's eye view of the project and bring value across the board.

A Kanban system also helps to shed light on previously invisible work. This helps to put finishing touches on all aspects of a project.

It is possible to incorporate the Kanban system in all types of organizations, and here are some of the things required.

- A whiteboard, some sticky notes, and magnets

- Work out expectations with the steering committee

- Explain to your team how simple project reporting will be and give them control

- Explain to them about certain metrics and trends and variances that might occur

- Explain how visualization can show them the real status of a project at a certain point in time

- Show your team how to work on Kanban using boards

- Tell them the importance of stop starting and start finishing

- Show them the importance of predictability and stability

## Is Kanban the Ultimate Solution?

No, Kanban cannot be viewed as an ultimate solution to problems. The best solution to bad project management is to lend more control and shift power into the hands of the project manager. Through the use of Kanban systems, a manager can control the outcome in a better way. This is especially relevant for companies that deal in complex projects that can find it a little tough to understand proper functioning of the project. The project manager will have to take care of many aspects associated with the project, including solving dilemmas and different complex situations that might arise. With the use of Kanban, all this can be resolved to a large extent.

## How Kanban Works

- Kanban helps to assign work and can be equally shared amongst members of the team. All members are required to manage their share of the work based on their preferences and priorities they set

- All member's progress can be viewed easily to understand where the problem lies and work on it to solve it

- If there are visual reminders of progress, then it is easy to know whether more members need to be added to the team to share the load, and it also becomes easier to know if any of the existing members need help or guidance

- Both individual and teams can be identified and measured using the same metrics on a Kanban board. It is ideal to make use of digital scales, as they can give you an accurate reading and also cut down on your input

- All members in the team will have access to whatever is going on in the organization and know exactly what another person is up to

Some project managers make the mistake of micro managing people. This means that they tend to over guide their employees owing to the power and control that they are given. This can lead to a lack of responsibility among employees. Employees might start feeling like they do not have to work hard and end up not contributing towards the end goal. All teams involved should make sure that they are well organized. They must plan their work out and understand what they have to do to reach the end goal. If the boss ends up micro managing every step of the way, then employees will not be able to work properly and will end up wasting their time and his.

## What You can Gain by Using Online Project Management Tools

If a project manager has access to online management tools, it will be easy for him to understand which team member is available and who is not. He can be up to date with the progress of the project. The tools can help to save the manager's time. He will know exactly how much time is being taken to complete the project. He can add comments, reviews, and analyze the project more easily. Online Kanban tools will help the manager reduce time spent on carrying out meetings and communications. These tools are especially useful for companies who work on large projects, as it can save them time and unify the different departments that are scattered all over.

## Why is Kanban so Effective?

Kanban systems are so effective owing to their simplicity. Team members and managers can easily list the tasks in the backlog or on the to-do list part of the board and choose the tasks that need attention immediately. They do not have to think about missing out on important tasks owing to excess workload.

If they are able to control the project, they will be satisfied with what they are doing. If a card is moved from the to-do list to the done list on the board, then it will feel good. This will motivate them to go after the other tasks and keep their teams motivated as well.

## What Makes Kanban Versatile?

Kanban tools can be quite versatile. They can be used across different departments and in different ways, as it is a very simple tool to use. There are only limited departments where Kanban cannot be adopted. It can easily fit into most departments. Kanban is mostly used in processes that can help to envision and make tiresome days less hectic and more organized. Managers and members who are part of the team will be able to plan their schedule in a better and more efficient way and understand if they have everything under control. If the project manager is under stress, all he has to do is look at the board and it will calm him down.

## How Visual Thinking Helps

As you know, it is much easier for a person to get a message if he has access to a picture compared to just words. Just by visualizing the flow of work, a person will be able to know exactly where a project stands. He will have access to the tasks that have been fulfilled and what needs to be done. As per studies, most people will automatically start visualizing tasks even if there are no visual cues. They will think visually and establish a structure that is well organized.

More and more businesses have now started to realize the value of using visual boards and are adopting Kanban systems. Regardless of their size and structure, they are taking Kanban systems on and using them to enhance their overall working. Looking at smaller teams and how they work will tell you how Kanban can be implemented. The team will start performing better and the organization will start looking for more ways to incorporate visual cues to finish the project on time. When knowledge about Kanban and its use goes around the organization, people will find it easier to implement it. They will be able to successfully incorporate it in their business.

If a team is looking to enhance its productivity, then here are some of the steps to follow.

- It is essential to not engage in multitasking, as it will prove to be a burden. Sometimes multitasking might be necessary but not always. There might be times when engaging in it might be useful, but if it is done regularly, then it will slow you down

- It is important to take breaks in between as it can help to reenergize and feel better. You will be able to work more freely and with a lot more enthusiasm

- The best thing to do is finish the toughest task first. It is important to go after tough tasks so that they can be done first, and you have enough time on your hands for other work

- Make sure you are not using your phone when working. Put it on silent mode

- Limit the number of meetings. Only call them if it is important

- Make sure you prioritize your tasks to ensure that the most important ones are tackled first

Kanban boards were first introduced to work in manufacturing forms, but will fit right into corporate offices. In fact, it will do best in project management. It can be used as a supplementary tool for others. They can be used to evaluate on-going projects and plan future ventures. By using Kanban boards, a company can increase its team's efficiency, maximize time available, and manage projects in a better way.

## Consistent Improvement

One big advantage associated with using Kanban boards is that they can help to instill continuous improvement. It is one where agile method can be beneficial in improving current conditions in the workplace.

Project managers and people who are working on the team will be able to review their progress consistently and be able to organize the work efficiently. They will also be prepared to respond to any changes.

Project managers can use the boards to not only simplify the projects but also address issues that are currently a part of the system. These issues might be posing a hindrance and stalling work. It is thus important to address the following aspects.

- Allocating resources

- Managing the workflow

- Identifying inefficiencies

By using online Kanban tools, it is possible to focus on functionality and versatility to supplement an existing project's tools. Kanban can help a team spend less time understanding a new system and focus more on going after its goals.

## Allocating Resources

Project managers make use of online Kanban tools to allocate resources and assign work to others. By allocating resources efficiently, project managers will be able to avoid any delays that might occur and deliver results on time. These resources can refer to on site members and off site members and third-party services. Here are the stages involved in resource allocation.

- Creation of work items

- Assigning work to team mates

- Collaborating with teams to prioritize work

Once a project has started, it is important to assess the progress on a regular basis to introduce any improvements. Kanban boards can help with this process such that every time a new project enters workflow, the right type of resource can be implemented in the best way.

## Workflow Management

Kanban boards will help project managers and their team to have a visual understanding of workflow. This workflow is nothing but a sequential flow of work or tasks. It refers to the order in which the task will move. There might be multiple tasks that are going on at once and should move in an orderly manner for the end goal to be achieved.

Using a visual representation of the different steps can serve as an indicator of how work is flowing. It will give us an understanding of the different elements involved and how they are working to help attain the end result. It can promote collaborations between different team members and departments. It will also help to find newer and better ways to solve any issues that might arise.

## Waste Reduction

Organizations that use lean usually tend to reduce costs by means of waste reduction. This waste is mostly from processes that are not efficient or a result of different opinions.

Waste can be in the following types:

### *Defects*
Defects refer to things that are not working properly as stated in business requirements.

### *Overproduction*
Overproduction refers to producing too much product and can result in throwing it away.

### *Idle Members*
Idle members refer to members whose work is delayed due to dependent tasks.

Kanban boards can be useful for project managers to find any issues or troublesome areas that might end up creating problems. Say for example cards are building up and creating a bottleneck. Team members will be given the task of getting rid of some of the load. This is especially important if the cards are causing a block or imposing impediments and preventing progress. These should be identified and rectified at the earliest so that they do not affect the final result. Once they have been addressed, people can go back to their previous tasks.

## Kanban Boards for Software Development

Software projects are usually complex in nature, and this can get to clients. It is especially annoying for those who are looking to finish fast. Kanban boards can provide visual relief and offer transparency to team members and stakeholders to follow.

Since Kanban boards are flexible in nature, they are quite popular among software developers who engage in repeated work techniques.

These repeated work techniques could make it easier by putting focus on certain aspects that can help to move the project forward. These are better known as minimum marketable features. When performed correctly, these satisfy a shareholder's expectations without delving into too much risk.

If a person goes beyond repeated processes, it can lead to backtracking. Some reasons include changes in technology, changes in objectives or goals, changes in the reach of the project, changes in its budget, or shifting focus from the project, amongst others.

As we know, project management should be flexible enough to adjust to changes. Working on iterated processes can help to reduce waste and remain more productive. There are high chances of avoiding issues that can crop up and ensure timely delivery of a project.

# Chapter Six

# Uses of Kanban Systems

Kanban refers to a software that is not just used on a whiteboard for listing out tasks using differently colored cards. It can do much more than that and help an organization in different ways, but it is important to stick with the principles laid down by the system.

As you know, Kanban is used in a plethora of industries, and its popularity is steadily on the rise. Right from established firms to start-ups, everybody is using Kanban to their advantage.

In this chapter, we will look at places where Kanban systems are most popular and the benefits they provide.

## Kanban in Software and IT

Now, you may wonder as to how Kanban can be implemented in software firms as it has its roots in the manufacturing industry. For this, we have to examine the differences between Kanban and other agile methods.

To start with, the main difference between Kanban systems and SCRUM is there is no time boxes in Kanban for tasks. The tasks that are a part of the Kanban system are larger and can be fewer in number. The time period assessment in Kanban systems are usually optional or there will be none at all. There is no speed of team in Kanban systems, and only the average time is assessed for implementation.

These specifications make us think what will remain of agile methods if all the main elements are removed. Increasing dimensions and reducing counting speed of a team will leave us with nothing. One will wonder as to how it is possible to consider supervision if the majority of tools have been taken out.

Most project managers tend to think about control and try to maintain it even when they do not have it. It is just a myth that a manager's supervision over development is mere fiction. If his team is not interested in working, the project is bound to fail even if he has full control over the team.

If the team is having fun when working on a project with proper efficiency, then there will be no need for control, as it will only increase costs.

Say, for example, one problem that is associated with SCRUM is the higher costs resulting from discussions and meetings and can end up leading to loss of time and at least one entire day being wasted to finish the sprint and another day to start the next one. If a sprint is two weeks, then two days out of two weeks is 20%, which is quite a lot. When using SCRUM, about 30 to 40% of time is wasted on supporting processes, such as daily rallies and sprint retrospectives, amongst others.

Kanban systems are different from SCRUM as they focus more on tasks. The main aim of Kanban systems is successfully completing a sprint. Tasks are the main focus. There is usually no sprint. The deployment is usually made when the completed work is ready for presentation. The team working on the tasks should avoid engaging in estimating the time taken to fulfill a task, as it can be incorrect and result in time wastage.

A manager should not worry about time estimates if he has faith in his team. The main objective of the manager is to prioritize tasks and fulfill objectives. That is his main job. There is no need for him to control anything else. The manager has to add items to the board based on their priority. This is the responsibility of a manager who adopts the Kanban system.

The team board of a Kanban system can look as follows. The following are placed from left to right.

### Goals

This is an optional column but will be quite useful on a Kanban board. Goals that are high level will be placed here so that everybody on the team will know what they are going after and have a constant visual reminder. Some examples include increasing work speed by 15% or the name of the task.

### Task Queue

Task queue refers to tasks that are ready to be started. The highest card that is placed in the queue is given top priority and is then moved to the next column.

### Acceptance

This acceptance column and the columns before the 'Done' column might vary based on how the work is flowing for the team. Tasks that are currently being carried out need to be finalized in this column. Once discussion about the same is done, it will be moved to the next column.

### Development

The task is maintained here until it is completed. Once done, it will be moved to the next column. If the structure of the task is not correct or it is somewhat uncertain then it can be moved back to this column.

### Test

The test column in a Kanban system is one where those projects are being mentioned that are being tested. If there are any issues in this column, the tasks are moved to the development column. If there are none, then they will be moved to the next column.

### Done

This section has cards of tasks that are completely finished. People do not have to worry about these tasks anymore. Priority tasks might also appear in this column. They are those that need to be performed on a priority basis. If the task needs immediate attention, it should be mentioned under "expedite" tasks. These must be completed as soon as possible.

We have discussed WIP limits throughout this book and why it is important for all managers to set WIP limits. Under each task that is pinned on the board, it is important to place a number, which will stand for the number of WIP tasks that can be assigned at any given point in time. These figures are usually chosen based on a team's capacity. A project manager will be aware of the numbers to be placed based on trial and error.

Say there are ten programmers who are a part of a project, the tasks under Development will carry a number between 4 and 5, depending on the team's capacity. This number has to be ideal, that is, not too small or too big. If it is too small, the team can get bored, and if it is too big then they might not be able to finish the tasks.

A good way of coming up with the right number is dividing the number of developers into a team of two and then coming up with a figure based on past project experiences.

Similarly, tasks have to be assigned for personnel belonging to other departments such as sales and marketing, amongst others.

## How Teams Benefit from Kanban

Here are some of the benefits that a team can derive by adopting the Kanban method.

To start with, it is important to reduce the number of tasks that are being performed at once in order to focus on finishing a majority. There will be no need to go into details of two or more tasks as it can lead to confusion. The manager will have planned the story queue, and all it takes for the team members is going through it to ensure that tasks are carried out on time.

Next up, tasks that are in the test column need to be addressed. As you know, not everything in the test column will end up being a success. Some of it can throw up problems. In such cases, you must work as a team to solve the problem. Once that is done, you can move the items to the next column.

Next, the time that is taken to finish a task has to be calculated. For this, the dates must be logged based on when a card was added to the task queue and when it was completed. The average waiting time will be calculated based on the time that was taken to finish a task. The manager or product owner will calculate this based on the figures at his or her disposal.

As we know, Kanban systems require a manager to adhere to a few basic principles, such as visualizing the product to divide the work into different tasks by placing colored cards on the board, limiting the WIP limit on each task at every subsequent stage of production, and measuring the cycle time to improve the processes involved, and to reduce the overall time. These are the basic terms of using Kanban, whereas when it comes to SCRUM, there can be nine terms, 13 terms in XP method, and 120 in RUP methods.

Kanban is not a project management or software development tool and does not tell people how projects should be carried out. It does not tell people how different processes should be planned and executed. It only provides a visual representation of the work and measures the progress of each team.

As opposed to SCRUM, Kanban can help to organize teams and improve their overall work. Microsoft has used Kanban since 2004 and has employed it in developing operations across the organization.

The best part of this system is that it can be applied to different departments and processes. If an organization is used to make use of agile techniques such as SCRUM and XP, or traditional ones such as waterfall, then Kanban can be extended to these methods to improve their overall functioning viz. quality of work, time taken to finish tasks, cycle times, etc. It can help the organization produce quality work in shorter periods of time.

## Kanban in Software or Product Development

Applications software development teams use Kanban to implement Agile and Lean principles. Kanban systems give teams certain principles and practices that can help them visualize their work and deliver quality results within short times. Teams who use these systems will have access to constant feedback that can help them improve their working standards. They will also have access to market research and customer likes, therefore further speeding up delivery times.

Kanban systems have evolved over the years and have become more adaptable to different industries. The IT industry has greatly benefited from it and continues to invite takers. It might take some time for a company to adopt the different aspects that are a part of the system, but once done, it will prove a good fit.

Kanban systems also provide teams with the necessary tools and techniques to improve their service level agreements and reduce the risk involved in processing and the cost of delay of delivering end products to customers within the right times. Kanban systems help delivery teams to match customer expectations.

Many businesses have now started to use Kanban for portfolio management. It can provide them with agility, and allows teams to perform tasks much faster.

## Kanban and Enterprise Agility

Kanban systems can help an organization enhance their delivery systems in order to deliver products easily and faster. This can be done by getting rid of obstacles and bottlenecks in the way. Workflow can be enhanced, and the time taken to deliver results will be much lower. It will be possible to obtain feedback from customers within shorter periods of time. This feedback can be used to enhance product output and service responsiveness.

Kanban systems help agile systems manifest teams and deliver products and services that are required by customers. The system aims to improve the way a company works.

Kanban systems are good for non-IT businesses too, as it was originally meant for the manufacturing industry. It helps to become lean and agile and produce high quality products. Both large and medium scale industries have been using lean Kanban systems to enhance their workflow and help the business, regardless of the type of products that they produce.

Kanban can be extended to multiple projects, such as engineering, insurance companies, legal firms, amongst others. We will look at them in detail in the next chapter.

## Tips to Choose the Right Kanban Software for Your Team

Here is some help for you to choose a software tool for your organization.

### *Flexibility and Scalability*

A small team is always more flexible and will do better with an informal Kanban system compared to a larger team. The same extends to the scale of the organization. It is best to look for software tools that are easier to use and can provide customizable features that accommodate a specific team's style of work. If the team plans to expand its work, then it is best to select a tool that can offer higher scalability.

## Collaboration

The Kanban system should always provide multiple features to share and collaborate with team members and stakeholders, and also customers. Tools that are easy to use and integrate features such as emails and exporting/importing data can help to secure information that is restricted and can also be shared across the board with team members, stakeholders, board members, etc. They can be assigned cards to send them notifications.

## Expandability

It is best to look for online Kanban system boards that look like physical boards. It will be easier to color code the boards using different cards. You can easily drop them into the appropriate columns. The tool you use should also allow you to add notes and images, as well as reports. There should be provisions to expand or extend the columns. Basically, you must be able to use the boards like physical boards. Right from checklists to tasks to images, you have to be able to add all of these to the virtual boards. It should also come with a due date feature so that you know exactly when to submit a project.

## Easy to Use

The software must be easy to use. A good Kanban software tool has to be easy to set up so that it is easier to start using it. There should be clear relevance between card data and spreadsheet columns. Members of the team should understand how they can implement the different features, such as emails, color-coding, and symbology, amongst others.

## WIP Limits

Team members have to be able to drag and drop cards between different columns in order to reflect their current work status and be within the prescribed WIP limits. If there are too many tasks that are a part of the workflow, then it might end up becoming too cumbersome. The chosen tool must allow you to move between the different columns and shift cards to match the specific set of data in order to provide a higher level of flexibility to the workflow.

### Metric Display

The chosen tool must include a feature that allows you to report, compile, and filter out information using cards and the spreadsheets. Some tools can also give you the option of charts and displaying high resolution colored cards, including Gantt charts that can add value to your systems.

### Integration

Integration is an important part of the process. Look for a software tool that is capable of letting you integrate with third-party software. For example, Jira's tracking software can help your team track the entries and find issues and duplicate entries. If you happen to use Google apps, then the software that can be used in tandem can help to reduce cycle times and match the software's calendar to Google calendar. If you happen to deal with other types of integrations, such as audio visuals, then it will be best to find systems that come with the features in-built so that you do not have to go searching for external software.

### Online Kanban Boards

If you feel like you need software that is constantly upgrading and can fit in well with your requirements, then you can go for online Kanban boards. There are many online Kanban boards to choose from; go for the ones that are a good fit for your company. Online boards are web-based boards or digital boards that can be used via phone and computers. They can be web-based or cloud based-that you can use to upload data. Some online boards come with many features, such as color coding, dragging and dropping, etc. Choose boards that allow you to instantly collaborate with team members. You always have the option of expanding virtual cards using logos and colors. It will be easier for you to view information by using metrics that are built into the system. Kanban boards can offer a variety of features that are all integrated within the software. Some online boards come with useful integrations, such as Jira's issue tracking, that can make it much easier for your team to process work.

## Benefits of Kanban Summarised

- With Kanban systems, you can always have shorter cycle times that can deliver different features much faster

- There will be a high degree of responsiveness to change

- When priorities change frequently, Kanban systems can prove to be the ideal choice

- It will be best to balance out the demand and meet customer requirements

- Kanban systems can provide a greater degree of flexibility

- It leaves more room to grow the company

- Kanban systems can help to reduce waste and get rid of activities that do not add value to the organization

- Kanban systems will allow rapid feedback motivation to members in order to empower them and allow them to perform better

## Disadvantages of Kanban

It would not be right to not discuss the disadvantages associated with the Kanban system, and some are as follows.

- The disadvantage of the Kanban system is that when there are radical shifts in demand, it can create an imbalance. It can create confusing signals that are tough to interpret. These fluctuations might be temporary in nature, but the effect they have on the system can be of a permanent nature, and thus, the board might have to be tweaked to match the current demand and how they can be effectively met

- To maintain quality, inventory levels are usually maintained at zero. Sometimes, inventory backup is needed to help against bad quality items, and thus it is important to have extra space in the warehouse for spare items that can be put to use in case there are issues

- Some personnel and teams might be averse to change and not adopt Kanban system efficiently

# Chapter Seven

# How to Use Kanban in Various Departments of an Organization

Kanban systems can be used throughout the organization. They can be a perfect fit for teams looking to collaborate. It is best for departments that are looking for cross-platform collaborations to enhance overall business. Using Kanban systems in different departments can help to identify the ways in which things can be improved by identifying and eliminating issues.

In this chapter, we will look at how Kanban systems can fit right into an organization and the different departments.

## Human Resources and Onboarding

Internal processes, including HR processes, can greatly benefit from Kanban boards, as they can help to organize various tasks. For example, the hiring system in a company. When companies put out ads for their openings, a lot of processes will begin, which are as follows.

- Many applicants will begin to get in touch with the HR team to enquire about the different openings based on the job description

- The HR department will have to gather the different applications that have come in, along with the resumés that are being mailed

- If the resumé meets the requisite criteria, the HR team will call up the applicants to talk to them in order to schedule interviews and go through the hiring process

All this can sometimes prove to be too much for the HR team, as they will have to keep up with too many people sending in their resumés, and tracking everything can end up being a headache. At this point, using a Kanban board can prove to be a great idea. The board can help to keep up with all the applications that are being sent in. the HR team will be aware of the different positions to fill and can start filling them in one by one based on the applications received and reviewed.

The HR team must deal with a lot of internal processes, such as onboarding, that can be dealt with efficiently using Kanban systems. Using visual aid can help to track new acquisitions. Kanban systems can work well with short-term projects that the HR department and the learning department have collaborated on.

## Purchasing Department

The Kanban system is ideal for the purchasing department, as the very word Kanban stands for billboards. Kanban systems were originally designed for purchasing teams and continue to be popular. It will work best in a purchasing, especially in import and export departments. Here is a look at how it works.

The team that manages the import and export department will process the different steps and use Kanban cards and Kanban boards to represent the processes visually. The different cards placed on the various columns represent the stage at which the process lies. This can be production, transit, and delivery. Kanban cards can help to visually represent processes, such as name and description of the products along with their value, weight and packaging, the date of arrival of the products, checklist of the different documents required for import or export, and a summary of the status of the products, etc. It always helps to have the board handy and keep it in the same room as the purchase manager. This can help to know how work is moving and prioritize tasks.

The various components involved have to be consumed within a period of time that is no longer than the lead-time. The supply of the source has to be capable of being able to produce larger quantity of the product in smaller amounts within a specific period of time.

A control cycle refers to a cycle that defines the different relationships that lie between the demand and the production line. The work area is the area where the demand for the material lies and the materials that are used for the production of various components.

The JIT, or just in time, is a signal that is generated in the system and will contain details such as the materials needed, the quantity needed, the date of delivery, the plant, the supply area that will receive the materials, the details of the vendors, amongst others . A scheduling agreement is one that is made with the vendor to supply the necessary materials for JIT. The Kanban quantity is the quantity that is allotted for Kanban systems that need to be filled once it has been emptied.

Kanban procedures refer to control over production and operational lines. Here are some of the types explained:

### Classic Kanban

This usually refers to procedures that can help to restock materials for the Kanban that are being circulated between the supply source and the demand source and the quantity per Kanban. As per this type of Kanban system, the number of Kanban being circulated is fixed or controlled, and the control cycle will signal the quantity of Kanban.

### Events Kanban

Events Kanban refers to the materials being used that are not available to the production and supply team. It is sourced once the materials have been requested. It will not depend on the number of Kanban present in the control cycle or the quantity in the cycle.

### One Card Kanban

These are used to restock when the Kanban from where material is being drawn is almost half empty. The new Kanban that comes must be restocked only after the current Kanban has been completely exhausted. This type is useful when materials are not required frequently.

### Kanban Quality Signals

Kanban quality signals refers to those where the signal will be made to the concerned departments when the quantity of Kanban has reached zero. The operator will make the signal as soon the quantity has reached zero in order for the stock to be replenished.

Most businesses will rely on shipments that are incoming, using Kanban cards and boards in order to track the different products coming in and going out. They can also be used to track products that are currently in use. The Kanban boards and cards can be used to signal all the individuals in the department know about the status of individual shipments.

Kanban boards usually offer department members an overview of all the things that are happening in terms of the shipment, and can decrease the need to check the files on a daily basis to assess the progress. This can help to increase productivity and help individuals know exactly when to expect the delivery of certain items. Shipments that have already been sent to the premise can be identified when the products are being taken out and exactly how they should be sent out to different departments.

## Development Department

Businesses that have a product development board can greatly benefit from using Kanban systems, as they offer a collaborative feature. Kanban systems help to carry projects faster and complete them on time.

It does not matter how big or small the project is, or whether it is being used by the development or the software team, the Kanban board is best for use in all types of development departments, as it can help to visualize the progress of the project and make changes if necessary. The systems can help for multiple reasons, but is mostly treated as a project management tool. It is important to understand that Kanban systems were originally designed for the manufacturing department, and thus its use in production, development, and assembly lines, remains quite popular.

The development team, known as the Dev team's work, is quite simple and straightforward. Overburdening them with complicated SCRUM can prove to be too much for them to handle. The use of SCRUM master and daily standups, meetings, planning, and sprint retrospectives, etc. will do well with SCRUM.

They can be simple to understand and visualize and know exactly what work has to be done in order to establish some common limits for WIP that can help to keep them going at a consistent pace using tailored Kanban systems.

But is it rare for Dev teams to have a straightforward solution at hand. It is often noticed that some projects will fit the bill making it easier to carry them out while some will need WIP limits and visualized flow to establish sense. The team has to assess the importance of the different processes involved and choose the best option available for the current situation.

## Operations Department

The operations department, unlike the production department, will need a Kanban system that is more flexible in nature. Operations will usually be large in capacity and require interruptive projects that can pop up throughout the day or week and come with different levels of prioritization and due dates.

The use of SCRUM will be based on the estimation of how much work will be done and the length of the sprint in the team. If there are too many ideologies that are being circulated, it can end up confusing the team and delay their work. Kanban systems will offer greater flexibility for any interruptions without any blockages and bottlenecks, and even prioritization will remain key.

Just by planning it out in advance, the operations team will be able to understand the Kanban board and determine what can be taken from the backlog. If something that is important pops up, it can be easily inserted back into the WIP columns based on the space that is available instead of waiting for the sprint.

This will help the operations team to respond better to the different issues that can affect the end user or to bugs that might be a part of the system.

If the organization has managed to implement DevOps, then it can be possible for the development operations to work smoothly using similar methods.

## The QA Teams

The quality assurance team relies on work being completed by the development team and those who are likely to be running with two or more different projects at different times. It can be tough to understand as to what the QA teams will work like when there are efficient and structured SCRUM teamwork. Kanban systems can make it easier for QA teams as their backlogs can be filled out by other teams. It will be important to maintain work efficiency that can allow QA teams to change up their priorities without unnecessary bottlenecks.

## Sales Team

When it comes to the sales team, it is important to remain as organized as possible. If there is disorganization, it will be quite difficult for the team to operate properly.

Kanban is nothing but an organizational system that delivers a just in time framework for companies to operate under. It was originally meant for the manufacturing team but quickly adopted by different departments, including the sales team. it serves as an ideal tool to organize and manage projects with greater efficiency. It can work well with the sales team. There are many Kanban systems to choose from including Trello and Zapier that can provide a plethora of options and integrations for the team to choose from.

Regardless of whether it is a big team or is operated by an individual, there will always be many tasks to take care of everyday a that need to be prioritized. Right from taking care of the meetings to calls and tending to emails, all tasks need to be prioritized to avoid an overburdening of information. It can make it difficult for the team to remain calm and process different information without getting confused. Most teams will stress out and end up delaying their work.

In such cases, it becomes important to remain organized and align different tasks with business cards in different columns. Each of the columns will contain specific cards having similar tasks say cards on the right side will be about prospects that are awaiting approval. All that the sales team has to do is accept new cards that are coming in and delegate them. If there is a need for it then the columns can be expanded, and new colored notes can be added to make the system more efficient.

Here is how it can work for them. A specific project enters a pipeline and is assigned a specific card that moves through the different stages. The number of WIP can vary depending on the project being carried out. A simple Kanban board can have the following mentioned on it: work to be completed, work in progress, work done, work in first contact, work in meeting, work in estimate, work in proposal presented, amongst others.

Since the board is easily available to everyone on the team, it is easy to assess the stage where the project lies. Kanban systems help people in the sales team to concentrate or focus on different tasks that are being carried out or the work in progress.

The basic principles can be applied easily across boards. Sales people usually require tools that can help them prioritize their work and ensure that things are well under control. They will enjoy their work only when they are focussed. Sales reps will be able to focus better on their work as they will be much more organized. There will be a system in place and they will not have to be worried about going through repetitive tasks and never-ending to-do lists. They can easily visualize their work and progress at any given moment in time. They will be better equipped to engage in WIP and not dwell on things that are not progressing. Focus will remain on tasks that are important, and they will put an end to multitasking.

Kanban system can serve as a tool for visualizing and tracking the different processes that lie across the Kanban boards. It is not just the sales department that can track their progress but also other departments. There will also be access to post sale activities and feedback and backlog loops.

Visual representation of all the information always makes it much easier for the team to plan out future sales. It will help them to understand and estimate the information and become more comfortable with using out of the box methods to capitalize on leads.

Kanban boards can help members remain engaged with sales in order to identify the different leads and move them to the next stage of the process. It can lead to colour coding that is easier to process and track movement across the board. It can give the team more information on leads and how to draw in more potential customers.

## Marketing Department

Regardless of the industry that you work for, if you are a part of the marketing team, then there is a chance of facing challenges that require you to meet stricter deadlines and execute the tasks that are multifaceted and urgent in nature. These projects can be quite demanding and require different phases to execute. Add to that the pressure of coordinating with your team and ensuring that nothing goes wrong. Since there is publicity involved, there will be a greater pressure to perform. It will come down to maintaining the image of the company. Events and media partners will have to be addressed and marketing strategies will have to be taken care of.

But with the use of Kanban, it is possible to visually represent the different processes and make sense of the chaos while trying to achieve larger goals. It will be possible to break down the different systems involved and make tracking easier. The marketing department will be able to communicate with the different levels involved and visualize the objectives as smaller fragments. There are always a few methods that can be employed to ensure that the entire structure is broken down properly. Kanban systems can prove to be quite an asset in this instance.

It can help to generate a landing page that caters to specific products. Here are some ways in which you can track the breakdown of your progress on a Kanban board.

Marketing teams have only recently started to officially adopt lean systems. Thus, mapping helps to connect different tasks on a Kanban board that are all connected to one another. When the tasks are all matched, it becomes easier for the teams to establish a relationship between the tasks and focus on the WIP limits to monitor the metric that is generated through the regular use of board visualization. Kanban systems can provide efficient methods for the entire process.

It is important to bear in mind that it is vital setting up systems to provide a visual representation of what is going on in the company and the progress of the different processes involved. It has nothing to do with the way in which your business has to be carried out. That is, the boards will not dictate the work and merely represent the progress of the work that is being carried out. Usually, you will not be required to change any of the processes involved, as it will become an iterative process and allow you and your team to achieve a greater level of productivity.

## Make a Master Portfolio

In order to make a master portfolio, a Kanban board can be used to track the status of different campaigns and the individual teams that are working on it and also the teams that have already worked on it.

The board can serve as a guide for your team to refer and track the cycle times of the campaign and any such information that are connected to the project. It can give them an in-depth view of the entire project and how things are progressing.

## Executing Work Breakdown

A daily work Kanban board can be used to track the individual campaign breakdowns and have a card or campaign portfolio to refer to in order to break the tasks down into smaller fragments that are connected. Say for example a campaign is used to build a launch page for a product, then the work to be carried out can be divided into smaller parts.

First off, the columns have to be labeled and the swim lanes on the board have to specify the different stages where the task lies and its connection with the overall context of the project. By using a master marketing board, it will be possible to track large scale objectives, such as ad campaigns and blog content along with advertisement campaigns and other aspects that are dependent on each other. Similarly, there must be a breakdown of the workflow so that it is easier to track the progress of the WIP. Master boards usually have process times that are simple and daily boards can follow the same structure.

Here is a look at the structure.

- Tasks that are ready to start or priority tasks and weekly meetings

- Tasks that are in progress and being carried out

- A review of work that has been carried out and the tasks that have been considered as completed but require feedback or inspection by a team lead

- Tracking the tasks that are dependent on external parties of teams that are involved in the campaign and other columns that can help to track progress

- When a task comes with two or more aspects that require the same time to finish, the team can split it into related tasks. Once the first task has been completed, it will be moved to the next task and signaled on the Kanban board

- It is important to move the tasks to the done column only after the work has been completed

## Task Dependencies in the Breakdown

Task breakdown is meant to understand the way in which a marketing campaign can be launched and the break down at the top level into the different parts. By mapping using a Kanban board, it is possible to breakdown the campaign but cannot be visualized with immediate effect. By using Kanban boards, work can be broken down and tracked using software. The breakdown of tasks will be represented using colored cards and establish a relationship between the various aspects involved. Tasks that are of the same level can be connected while those that are larger will end up becoming parents to smaller tasks.

By making links between the colored cards, it will be easier for a parent to show a child the relationship that exists between them and a relative. Similarly, tasks can be interconnected using the cards. It will be easier to break down the hierarchy that exists between the top level and subsequent tasks. The relationship and the progress can be monitored. Using Kanban boards, it will be easier to visualize the breakdown of the work involved across the board by using analytical modes that can create a visual representation of the relationship that exists within the structure. The links between the tasks can be created by breaking down the entire structure and monitoring progress. It can be tracked down through the course of the project by using visual boards and analytical modules that are available across the board to all departments.

## Assigning Tasks to Individuals and Not Groups

When it comes to large scale marketing teams, where more than two people are involved, it becomes quite difficult to track and breakdown the tasks. In such instances, there is always a danger of tasks not being assigned responsibly. For this reason, when tasks are being created, the breakdown is planned out by assigning basic level tasks to different members of the team. For example, if the launch page is to be created, a copywriter and a team lead will be assigned the task. Along with them, a third person has to be assigned to serve as a coordinator or supervisor just to ensure that the task is being carried out efficiently.

By making use of the software, it will be easier to break down the tasks and assign different tasks to people across the board. For example, in the launch page task, the copywriter will take on the role of the assignee and the designer will be the copywriter's assistant. A project manager will be overlooking all the processes that are involved and each of the tasks will be assigned to individuals in order to complete the puzzle.

## Tracking Time is Important

When it comes to marketing, it is important to be at the right place at the right time. When campaigning, is essential to for the marketing team to know exactly where their team is headed to understand how their campaign will go. Data that will be acquired during the campaigning process will be after the campaign's process. Kanban cards can help to track individual tasks in order to come up with estimates for future projects and track how well the campaign is moving.

It is important to look at the different details and the manpower required for different items, the cycle times, and lead times for projects of all sizes. Cycle times are nothing but a way of measuring the time it can take to finish a task from when it is placed on the WIP column until it is moved to the Done column on the Kanban board. The budgets set aside for the projects will not be calculated based on the financial situation alone, but also on resources and commodities.

It is important to keep track of time-based metrics in the graphics for cycle times to show how much time it will take for a team to finish different tasks.

The marketing team can go a little further to evaluate the trends and flow charts to assess the workflow and gather information that pertains to the individuals and their teams. This information can be used to assign tasks and break them down effectively. Marketing teams are advised to have meetings at least once a month so that they can go through progress and come up with analytical visualizations of the acquired data that has been accumulated about individual teams based on the week and share it with people on the team.

## Staying Lean

By breaking down the marketing campaign using a Kanban board and adopting the lean method, it will be easier to manage and execute the project. It will take some time and effort, but you will get better at it by adopting a dedicated tracking system. You will be able to track your team's progress and how they have been performing and go for similar results.

Kanban boards can help with a lot of things when it comes to the marketing department. Sometimes, companies can have many different marketing departments. If they are not on the same page, it can lead to fights and discrepancies. For this, Kanban boards can be used to unify the different departments and put them on the same page. Here are some of the aspects that the teams have to take care of in general.

- SEO management and content marketing

- Social media marketing

- Video Marketing

- Email Marketing

- Print Advertisements

- Connect with potential agencies

- Connect with media or channels

These are the prime tasks assigned to the marketing department and must be carried out every time a campaign is announced. Kanban boards can be used to keep track of these and organize different aspects. The marketing team can come up with a more organized list. Here are some things to mention on the list.

- What tasks are in the backlog or inventory list?

- What are some of the tasks that are currently running?

- How fast can the tasks be completed?

- What are the next set of tasks

If the marketing department wants to make use of a board to measure the different metrics involved, it can add more columns to the board to answer the following questions.

- What is working for the department?

- What is not working for the department?

- What tasks are not going to plan?

- What aspects need to be adjusted?

It is the manager's job to find the different areas where efforts must be made to focus on the areas that need attention in order for the work to be completed on time.

## Customer Support Department

Kanban boards have been in use in almost all departments of an organization, and continue to be popular. It is easy to implement the boards in IT departments, sales, purchases, marketing, and also customer support. Those who have used the board for this purpose will vouch for the fact that it is extremely easy to use it and can greatly enhance work experience.

Kanban systems help customer service personnel to be more efficient and remain organized to deliver the best support to customers. The time taken to respond, and the quality of service provided, would both be much better. Kanban tools can help personnel remain organized based on the feedback received from customers, any problems that arise, and suggestions that have been made. Virtual Kanban boards can help them communicate with other departments so that it is easier to solve customer queries.

One issue that is common in the customer support department is managing many tickets that should be replied to in order to keep customers happy. Most of them must be addressed within 12 hours, and this can prove to be a herculean task owing to the number of complaints that can be raised. All of them have to be given the same level of importance, and guarantee the customers that their queries will be answered as soon as possible without delay. They should be promised an experience that is free from issues and errors. The visualizations provided by Kanban boards help to access the different tickets easily so that each one can be addressed one after the other.

A lot of the issues or tickets are stored in emails. After a while, it can become cumbersome. For this, it is best to rely on Kanban boards where it is much easier to maintain the tickets and can be classified based on the level of urgency. It will be more manageable and easier to access. Kanban boards can help to categorize the different tickets according to preset metrics.

Not all tickets can be resolved by the ticket team; some need to be forwarded to specific departments. For this, the different departments will be notified as soon as a ticket is raised. Good Kanban systems, such as Zapier, can help here as the query can be sent to a specific department.

Zapier offers quite a lot of features, such as email scanning, tagging, and providing feedback, suggestions, answering queries, etc. Each of these can create a new Kanban card on the board and carry specific information pertaining to the issue that has been raised or the information that has been requested. The user account domain is present on the top left of the card, along with an ID for the tasks to help the support and customers know how the ticket is progressing.

This makes it extremely easy for both parties to keep track of tickets. All it takes is one to know what is happening. This can reduce the time and effort required to solve issues. Different colored cards are used to signal the progress of tickets. For example, red cards for those that are yet to be resolved and green for resolved cards. Blue cards can signify feedback and suggestions.

However, there might be limitations involved, as technology needs constant upgrading. There might be a BUG in the reports that has to be resolved as soon as it arises. There should not be too many tickets waiting in the BUG area or the WIP area of the board. They should be pulled to the 'Done' column as soon as they are solved. New tickets should not be taken until some of the tickets in the WIP area have been addressed. If some tickets need support, the concerned department should be addressed immediately in order to solve the issue faster. The departments should be limited to no more than two tickets at one time. As soon as the ticket has been resolved, it should be forwarded to customers so that they know about the decision before it is moved to the resolved column. This section requires a good amount of communication and collaboration in order to fasten the process. It is possible to enable email notifications if you want to be sure about having reached a solution for a specific ticket.

Kanban tools can help to fulfill the role of a feedback column. Suggestions, feedback, requests and contact details can all be filled and submitted using Kanban boards. It will be easy to retrieve this information for later reference. Having a contact column will make it much easier for people to revert back with queries and reminders. It will always help the support team benefit.

## Helpdesk and IT Department

Support tickets usually tend to flood help desks, but with the use of Kanban boards, it is easy to organize the different tickets based on priority and move them to the different columns based on their urgency. Using Kanban software can be quite easy and help different departments function optimally. They can use differently colored cards to organize data. This system can help address issues that have been raised and implement strategies to prevent them from cropping up again. The department can work on finding solutions to the issues to enhance their performance and cut down on errors.

## Operations Department

As you know, different departments that are a part of the business represent different areas of the whole structure. All of them should come together to work as one and remain accountable for the entire company's function. As Kanban boards help all departments to look at how they are doing with work, it can help them and make sure they are on the right track and working in tandem with different departments. Kanban boards provide the best means of connecting different departments together and can be used to find how work is flowing.

## Forecasting Using Kanban Boards

Based on how organizations make use of Kanban, the company will be able to predict work for the next three to four weeks by using the right tools. If tools are implemented efficiently, it will be quite easy for the organization to forecast the entire project. Here is a look at it in detail.

## Forecasting of Single Features

Companies that tend to push the processes over into development lines are under the assumption that the processes will be completed eventually. They will not be in a position to assess the capacity of the members involved in the development team. Companies usually forget that systems slow down when bottlenecks occur and lead to mistakes and delays.

Therefore, unless relevant data is collected to feed into a prediction system, organizations will not be able to end this vicious cycle. And it is not just the company that can benefit from it but also customers and stakeholders who have access to information that will tell them where the organization is headed. Development teams too will benefit from it, as they will have access to the different tasks that are being moved from one department to another.

If the work is not being assigned properly, it will lead to bottlenecks and unpredictable systems that cannot give an accurate understanding of how the project is moving.

Organizations that use Kanban systems for at least three weeks will have enough data at their disposal to map a lead-time histogram. This can help an organization have an accurate prediction for the near future, but it is important for an organization to not get into forecasting too soon. It can end up forgoing opportunities to achieve something bigger and better.

If an organization is beginning to collect data for predictions, the following questions have to be answered.

- When can this task start?

- Should this task be momentarily stopped to start another important one?

- Is it too late to start this task?

- Are there risks involved in delaying this task?

- If risks are too high is it best to ignore the tasks?

- If the task is delayed, how much will it cost?

## Forecasting of Multiple Features

Similarly, Kanban boards can be used to forecast for multiple features. There are many different types of tools and simulators that cater to this type of prediction. Some of them include the Monte Carlo simulation that can be used to calculate the probabilities that are associated with the different sets of data available.

## Back Offices

It is essential to understand that Kaizen is not a tool that is used with Kanban; it is the other way around. Kanban is a tool that is used by both individuals and companies to remain organized with their work and efficiently finish all the tasks at hand. This makes it a versatile tool to implement in all departments of the company, but how will it fit into the back office? Well, let us find out.

To start off, think of the most important thing that must be done in an organization. All the tasks that are sketched out for the day have to be carried out efficiently. As soon as the day begins, the list is pulled out by the individual departments and the tasks are addressed one by one. It is important to go on in an orderly fashion and tasks have to be completed one after another.

This is where Kanban steps in. It helps to organize tasks and get rid of unnecessary clutter and clumping of tasks. There might be times when tasks go unnoticed if task lists are being maintained in the head. With the help of Kanban boards, this can be avoided, as it will be difficult to miss out on tasks, as they will be clearly mentioned on the board. It will be possible to classify tasks based on their level of importance and place them in columns such as priority and urgency. This will ensure that the important tasks are addressed first before moving to the next ones.

However, if there are too many roadblocks or bottlenecks, then the team can move to the next task and leave the current one as it is. Kanban is all about finishing instead of starting. At some point the team will realize that there is a lot of work that has been left halfway, and start finishing it one by one. The team will go through the WIP columns and start moving the items to the 'Done' columns. Say for example the marketing team reaches the office at 10am. They have a 6pm deadline and end up having a backlog of tasks that they started at various points of the day but did not complete. At about 5pm a new and important task comes along that simply must be started. They decide to take the help of another marketing team in the company, but they too are busy with an important task, and taking this up might create a backlog for them.

This issue can be resolved through the use of Kanban systems. Here is how it can be done.

All individuals who are part of the team must take up and finish a task and stick with it until it is finished. If the tasks are too many, then one individual can take two or three at a time and make sure they finish them within the stipulated period of time. This will ensure that they focus on the task at hand. If the backlog is small, then all the individuals will have to go through lesser obstacles while finishing the tasks

When the next task is assigned to the team, members need to ask the following questions:

- Is this a high priority task?

- Why should this task be completed?

- What benefits can be derived by completing this task?

- Who will benefit from this task?

These questions will help the team to assess the importance of a task and how soon it should be completed. It will also tell them how to value different tasks.

Kanban systems help employees to add more value to their tasks. The main aim of the system is to help individuals perform at least one task that will add to the overall team's value. This means that it is important to set a high bar for all the members who work towards the end goal. Most organizations that implement Kanban use agile systems. Teams put their workflow on the Kanban board and assess the different tasks that need to be completed through the course of the day or week. They will use visual cues to identify and get over obstacles that might come their way. The systems will not be able to get over the bottlenecks and can end up crowding the team member's desk.

The board will also not be able to tell whether the task of being carried out can add any value to the whole project. Managers will prefer to use the Kanban system as they can be in control of the entire process from start to finish and exercise greater control in team members. It is important to keep the following things in mind:

- Following the real demand of customers

- Lowering the backlog at hand

- Speeding production flow

Kanban systems will not function without lean management. Teams can improve their working over several years but the tools to assess the real value add to the overall functioning of the team. Kanban systems must be able to assess the value of the product or service that is being put out whether or not it has helped team members to effectively finish work by eliminating backlogs. Organizations tend to use lean tools without fully exploiting their full potential. It can be a challenge to understand the different functions that they provide and then implement them in the organization.

## Why Use Kanban Tools?

By now, you understand the actual use of having a Kanban system in your workplace. Not only can it provide visual management, but it also allows you to have a customized board to carry out everyday work more efficiently. Here is a look at the different benefits associated with using Kanban boards in the workplace.

### *Data Stored Clearly*

Kanban boards can help you remain more organized and make it much easier for you to go through the content to find specific items. By integrating emails with Kanban boards, it will be easier to receive inbox mails and integrate them into the working space.

### *Easy to Navigate*

Using an email system to store data can make it quite difficult to manage. It will be important to have an organized system that can help to control an overflow of data and categorize them in such a way that is easier to access without much effort. Personnel from different departments will not be overwhelmed at the prospect of the lots of information coming their way.

## Collaboration

Using Kanban systems can make it much easier for different departments to collaborate with each other. The basic use of the board is to receive queries and issues and respond with solutions. Right from the IT department to the marketing department, to sales to purchases, all departments can connect with each other and establish a cross department connection. WIP will be limited and efficient solutions will be devised for different issues.

## Automation

Kanban boards promote automation. This means that it will be easier for people to integrate different aspects such as emails, calendars, etc. With the use of color co-ordination cards, people can store and access data with just one click. Kanban systems can help customer support teams answer customer queries and solve their tickets faster. It is also possible to have instant feedback.

As you can see, there are many advantages associated with using Kanban systems in the organization. It will fit into any department and make it easy to carry out work. As soon as work is done, it can be moved from one column to the next, and so on.

# Chapter Eight

# How can Kanban Help in Legal Department

It is possible to adopt the Kanban system in the legal department. It can help to drive the business and transform the department.

Kanban and agile methods can be implemented within legal firms. It will be important to find a software that are good for the organization as a whole and the different teams that are involved. If you wish to find the best systems for your team then look for an agile coach who can advise you on the best system to adopt.

It is obvious that most organizations do not accept change wholeheartedly and law firms will especially be averse to tasking risks. It is not fair to burden the team with a new system that is different from what they are used to using. The desire for the organization to excel can make them adopt the system and implement it across different departments.

Some organizations will be looking to drive change into the systems and aim for achieving excellent results. These can be hampered due to an overburdening of information and a lack of compartmentalization that can lead to restricted workflow.

It is important to understand the basics of agile methods, in this case so that it is easy to implement Kanban systems. If all members are made aware of the system and what it has to offer, it can help to transform the way in which the organization operates.

It can take some time for members to accept the new system and adopt it to maximize gains and allow the results to last long. A coach can help you understand the different systems that are available and what each one can offer. You can consider visiting workshops to better understand the concept and what will best suit the needs of the legal department.

Understanding the basics of agile principles and how implementing them can help your organization remain more organized and put out better services will help to implement the concept faster. Again, it will be best to educate everyone involved about the concept so that it is easier to adopt it and set aside the aversion to change.

Kanban boards can be used by teams to come up with schedules for meetings, to-do lists and names of members who will be a part of the team. This will make it easier for the team to know exactly what it is that they have to be doing and the due date for each task. There will be a lot of transparency involved and team members will be able to work to their full potential. They will be able to monitor to progress and whether the project is going according to plan.

Kanban systems can help the team to find duplicate work and how certain pre-existing work results can be used by other teams to save time and establish consistency. Organizing feedbacks can ensure that team members are given the platform and the chance to understand how things work and the way in which it is carried out. Kanban systems helps to establish uniformity and make sure that everybody is treated equally.

It is obvious that the organization will require a lot of change to be introduced and will not be an easy task. It can get a little frustrating to adopt a lot of change within a short period of time. It will require some feedback sessions and patience for the system to work efficiently. There will be some level of planning involved and important for all the team members to take part in it. Sometimes, the same type of issues can tend to arise, and the best way to deal with it is by making sure the root cause is addressed. Employing a team to assess the areas where there is some degree of resistance can help to fix the issues at heart.

Again, if you have a coach assisting you then they might be able to provide the solution to the issue.

In case something does not go according to plan then it is best to switch to a backup plan so that it will not only be easy for team members to adopt to the systems but also easier for the organization to get projects going.

Once the systems have been set up, it should not take the teams any more than ten minutes to change the board and make it up to date. Tasks that were personalized in backlogs can be prioritized and made available to the next team that will be working on it. It will be important to assess the skills and experiences of the team members handling the boards and deciding the priorities to attain best results.

Kanban systems can help develop cross-functional skills for high demand jobs and help different teams pull together to finish urgent tasks. If there are important tickets to be resolved, someone or other from the team can work to resolve it.

As is the case with most organizations that adopt Kanban systems, it will be important to introduce WIP limits, better known as work in progress limits, to ensure that teams are not working on too many tasks at one time. This can slow them down and affect their output. Teams will start to focus more on the actual business and personnel belongings ad will be able to find the tasks that have to be finished first in order to add more value to the overall project.

Kanban systems can help legal forms become faster, in terms of doing the right thing, and better, by giving advice and tailor-made results. Real teams will be able to communicate better and solve challenges that are posed by the business.

Colleagues can step up to solve each other's issues and help to establish a supportive and friendly work environment. It will be easier for the team to accept change compared to individuals going about it.

Agile methods can greatly help legal professionals as they can help to cope with complexities associated with the business. Giving legal advice to businesses can be a complex task, and tasks such as drafting agreements and engaging in M and A activities can do well by employing the correct people at the right times, but this can often be tough to manage and happen in agile systems and self-organizing teams.

Therefore, if the basic business that the law firm uses multidisciplinary approaches and requires a greater degree of teamwork then agile methods can prove to the best choice. Systems can bring real advantages and establish better workflow based on the information and lead to better co-operation between various boards to contribute to the end goal. Agile methods can also help to distribute the work in a more even way and ensure the right work is going into the hands of the right people, but it is important to understand that agile cannot be an on and off process, and has to be performed consistently so that results are even. Both in-house and lawyers who practice privately can make use of agile systems.

It is best for teams wanting to adopt the system to understand organizational agility and a shift in the mindset of individuals to go from being managers to leaders. It is important to find an approach that can suit the individuals, and also the organization as a whole. There can be different ways in which the organization can adopt agile methods and remain committed to it to bring permanent change to the system.

Having Kanban systems can help law firms become better and cope with changes in the environment and the various demands associated with it. Most lawyers will be used to this; it will be important to filter in change gradually.

As mentioned earlier, it is best to consult an agile coach who will be able to suggest a tailor-made system to suit your firm's needs. It is best to stick with a simple plan at first so that it is easy to implement it and ensure that the system is best suited.

Having a goal-oriented approach can let your organization adopt agile and managers will be able to better delegate work to the right personnel. Decision-making will be easier, and teams will be able to adapt to the iterative processes. It can be a less stressful experience and make it easier for teams to adopt and implement Kanban boards every step of the way.

A lot of lawyers end up doing basic tasks, such as editing and synchronizing copies and other such work. Through the use of Kanban systems, it is easier to achieve simple changes by adopting cloud-computing methods. This means that staff will be able to collaborate and share the same documents and avoid duplication. It will be possible to integrate tracking software that can help to enhance business opportunities.

Some systems, such as Jira and electronic Kanban boards, can help to spread projects information across the various branches of the firm regardless of how far away they are located. The systems can help to merge the different pieces and provide a more cohesive platform. Say a ticket is created, and it needs information from a certain email or draft, it will be possible to have everything in one place through integration and the person working on the ticket needs not go to ten different places and have it all in one place.

Contract generation tools can help businesses create drafts and not have to bother about running them through legal languages or having to revert back to the legal department. This can save time and effort and help deliver seamless service at a faster pace.

By combining this with a reporting system it can showcase the accepted level of risk, it will be much easier and faster to get through tickets. There can be many tools that can be integrated into the chosen Kanban system and make it easy for the firm and lawyers to carry out their work.

# Conclusion

I thank you once again for choosing this book and hope you found it informative and interesting.

Kanban systems were built in the 1940s by Taiichi Ohno for Toyota. The technique was then adopted by several organizations more prominently in 2004 by David Anderson for IT companies to enhance their overall functioning.

Using Kanban systems can help an organization identify different tasks that have to be finished to complete a project. The Kanban board will be used to mention the different processes and mention the stage at which it is. It will help teams to find any obstacles or bottlenecks and ways to solve them to forward the project to the next stage.

I urge you to go through this book to understand the basics of Kanban once again. The system will help you not only finish the tasks that you have started but also deliver better end products on time. It can also help to forecast future projects by using statistical tools.

It can help organizations maintain transparency and connect different departments with each other for cross department collaborations.

I hope you have a good time adopting Kanban systems in your organization.

# Sources

https://www.digite.com/kanban/what-is-kanban/

https://www.smartsheet.com/understanding-kanban-inventory-management-and-its-uses-across-multiple-industries

https://www.leonardogroupamericas.com/go/index.php/manufacturing-blog/94-is-kanban-obsolete

https://www.digite.com/blog/has-kanban-truly-arrived-for-project-management/

https://gerardchiva.com/2017/01/21/predictability-in-kanban-systems/

http://www.djaa.com/project-management-kanban-part-3-forecasting

https://news.ibqmi.org/six-types-of-kanban-explained

https://www.leankor.com/what-departments-can-use-kanban-boards/

https://www.lean.org/balle/DisplayObject.cfm?o=3298

https://leankanban.com/kanbans-change-management-principles/

https://www.graphicproducts.com/articles/kanban-benefits/

https://blog.crisp.se/2013/10/21/mattiasskarin/enterprise-kanban-improving-the-full-value-chain-using-lean-thinking

https://dzone.com/articles/working-with-kanban-frequently-asked-questions

http://blog.debugme.eu/history-of-the-kanban-method/

https://tallyfy.com/kanban-system/

https://zapier.com/learn/project-management/kanban-board/#basics

http://leanmanufacturingtools.org/kanban/

file:///C:/Users/ADMIN/Downloads/Presentation-Withdrawal-
Production-and-Supplier-the-Three-Types-of-Kanban.pdf

https://medium.com/@digite/implementing-a-successful-kanban-
system-for-manufacturing-and-inventory-management-
be6d27147986

https://leankit.com/blog/2017/03/6-benefits-kanban-project-
management/

https://techbeacon.com/why-you-should-use-kanban-project-
management

https://leankit.com/learn/kanban/kanban-boards-for-project-
management/

https://www.sitepoint.com/how-why-to-use-the-kanban-methodology-
for-software-development/

https://www.allbusiness.com/kanban-can-help-take-stress-sales-
106997-1.html

https://kanbanize.com/kanban-resources/case-studies/break-down-and-
track-your-marketing-campaign-with-kanban/

https://kanbantool.com/use-cases/kanban-in-customer-service/support-
team

https://blogs.sap.com/2015/03/20/kanban-process-for-external-
procurement/

https://www.cprime.com/2015/04/3-departments-that-could-benefit-
from-kanban/

https://legaltrek.com/blog/2016/06/agile-law-how-to-apply-kanban-in-
a-legal-department/

Made in the USA
Monee, IL
15 December 2023